# MANAGE YOU

# About the Author

Brian Sutton is a Human Resources Consultant who provides outplacement services and HR advice and guidance to organisations in both the public and private sectors. He previously held HR appointments with an engineering company in the North-West, a major manufacturer in the building industry and the UK's largest motoring organisation.

A Fellow of the Institute of Personnel and Development, Brian has an extensive background in Human Resources at both a strategic and operational level. His widespread experience of managing complex people issues has given him a profound appreciation of the factors affecting human behaviour in individuals faced with making major decisions about their career.

# MANAGE YOUR CAREER

## The Definitive Guide to Successful Job Search and Career Change

## BRIAN SUTTON

Arrow
**BUSINESS BOOKS**

Arrow Books Limited 1998

1 3 5 7 9 10 8 6 4 2

© Brian Sutton 1998

Brian Sutton has asserted his rights under the Copyright, Designs and Patents Act, 1988 to be identified as the author of this work.

This book is sold subject to the condition that it shall not, by way of trade or otherwise, be lent, resold, hired out or otherwise circulated without the publisher's prior consent in any form of binding or cover other than that in which it is published and without a similar condition including this condition being imposed on the subsequent purchaser.

Arrow Books Limited
20 Vauxhall Bridge Road, London SW1V 2SA

Random House Australia (Pty) Limited
20 Alfred Street, Milsons Point,
Sydney, New South Wales 2061, Australia

Random House New Zealand Limited
18 Poland Road, Glenfield
Auckland 10, New Zealand

Random House South Africa (Pty) Limited
Endulini, 5a Jubilee Road, Parktown 2193, South Africa

Random House UK Limited Reg. No. 954009

Papers used by Random House UK Ltd are natural, recyclable products made from wood grown in sustainable forests. The manufacturing processes conform to the environmental regulations of the country of origin.

---

Companies, institutions and other organizations wishing to make bulk purchases of any business books published by Random House should contact their local bookstore or Random House direct:
Special Sales Director
Random House
20 Vauxhall Bridge Road
London SW1V 2SA
Tel: 0171 840 8470 Fax: 0171 828 6681
www.randomhouse.co.uk
businessbooks@randomhouse.co.uk

---

Typeset by SX Composing DTP, Rayleigh, Essex
Printed and bound in Great Britain by
Cox & Wyman, Reading, Berks

ISBN 0 09 927228 8

'One can't believe impossible things,' said Alice.
'I daresay you haven't had much practice,' said the Queen.
'When I was your age, I always did it for half-an-hour a day.
Why sometimes I've believed as many as six impossible
things before breakfast.'

*Alice in Wonderland* – Lewis Carroll

# Contents

Acknowledgements — xi

## Part One – Making An Adjustment

Chapter 1   Introduction   3

Chapter 2   The Importance of Positive Thinking   7

Chapter 3   Redundancy – Facing up to the Future   11

*What is redundancy? • The feelings you encounter • Making the best of a difficult situation • Rights of redundant employees • Taking care of yourself • Personal finance • A friend in need*

Chapter 4   More of the Same? Or Time for a Change?   35

*Self-assessment • Are you in a rut? • Employment trends • Choosing a job where maturity is valued • Examine your finances • Involving your partner • Moving house • Status • Salary and benefits • Where can you use your skills? • Your health • Change to what?*

| | | |
|---|---|---|
| Chapter 5 | The Importance of Knowing Yourself | 49 |

*Transferable skills • Types of skill • Ranking your skills • Fleshing out your skills • Strengths v weaknesses • Searching for other strengths*

# Part Two – Getting The Job You Want

| | | |
|---|---|---|
| Chapter 6 | Planning for Success | 59 |

*Getting a job is a job in itself • From your personal viewpoint • Space of your own • Establishing an office routine*

| | | |
|---|---|---|
| Chapter 7 | Researching the Job Market | 65 |

*Identifying potential employers • PC information on employers*

| | | |
|---|---|---|
| Chapter 8 | Compiling Your Curriculum Vitae | 71 |

*Which CVs win interviews • The personal profile • How to make a start with achievements • Other useful tips • Leisure interests • CV presentation • Technology in selection • The final word*

| | | |
|---|---|---|
| Chapter 9 | Vacancies – How and Where to Find Them | 89 |

*Advertised vacancies • The Internet • Recruitment specialists • Outplacement services • Jobcentres • Computerised registers • Exhibitions • TV and radio • Professional associations • Networking*

| Chapter 10 | The Art of Networking | 105 |

*What is networking? • The correct networking technique • Networking letters • Networking meetings*

| Chapter 11 | Responding to Advertised Vacancies | 111 |

*What to look for in advertisements • Ageism • Other points to look for • Application letters • Application forms*

| Chapter 12 | Making Speculative Applications | 129 |

*Speculative letters to recruitment specialists • Speculative letters to employers*

| Chapter 13 | Winning at Interviews | 137 |

*Interviews with consultants • Interviews with employers • A well-structured interview • Preparing for your interview • The interviewer's questioning technique • Interview questions most commonly asked • Some crucial questions • Questions which you should ask • Controlling interview nerves • Appearance • Body language • On the day of the interview • Reviewing your performance*

| Chapter 14 | Other Selection Methods | 173 |

*Selection tests • Assessment centres • Job simulations • Graphology*

| Chapter 15 | Coping with Rejection and the Job Offer | 183 |
|---|---|---|
| | *After the interview • Coping with rejection • The job offer* | |
| Chapter 16 | Working for Yourself | 187 |
| | *Do you have what it takes? • Advice and guidance • The business plan • Legal identities • Franchising* | |
| Chapter 17 | Useful Sources of Information | 195 |
| | *Careers • Job search • National newspaper advertisements • Interim Management • Self-employment • The voluntary sector • Further education • Employment advice • Pensions, investments and financial planning • Benefits and entitlements • Taxation • Health* | |
| | **Index** | **207** |

# Acknowledgements

No one writes alone and many people and experiences have shaped my thinking and approach to this publication. Pride of place belongs to my wife Jacquey. Her good humour, understanding and sharp eye for detail has kept me on the straight and narrow. In addition, I have been blessed with a capable team of supporters who have given their time to help edit and offer advice.

# Part One

# MAKING AN ADJUSTMENT

# 1
# Introduction

*'Distance doesn't matter; it is only the first step that is difficult.'*
Marquise du Deffand

You are probably reading this book because you're actively looking for a job or perhaps thinking of doing so.

Job hunters come in different guises, their career moves a haphazard process often caused by negative events. On a positive note, you may feel dissatisfied with your current promotion prospects or maybe your employer hasn't recognised your worth in terms of pay and benefits. You could be simply bored with the same routine or feel you've been in the wrong job for years and want to do something new. Perhaps your health has deteriorated and you need something less physically demanding. However, you may have no choice in the matter as change is being forced on you because of redundancy. You may be a school leaver or a graduate looking for your first job, or someone who is seeking their next job as part of a well laid out career plan.

Why do you need a book such as this to help you find a job? If your need for a career move has been brought about by one of the negative events mentioned above, then very often these can cloud the issue, making it difficult for your approach to be rational and decisive without professional support.

Successful job-hunting, like anything in life, can only be achieved if you are prepared to work at it. Job-hunting is often said to be a lonely experience, so to set out on your own, without the benefit of professional support and advice, is to risk encountering ongoing rejection and disappointment that may lead you to simply abandon your search before a job is found.

Looking for a new job or a change of career is full of pitfalls for the inexperienced. If you have not been in the job market for some time, your job search skills will have become blunted.

Of course this book won't get you a job – only you can do that – but by taking onboard the advice it contains you stand a much better chance of succeeding.

As the author of this book, my own career takes in 25 years' experience of recruitment and selection as part of a broad human resources background, together with outplacement, career counselling and consultancy. During this time, I have handled countless CVs, conducted thousands of interviews and given face-to-face career advice to a great many people.

This experience leads me to conclude that a large number of those in pursuit of their next career move have little or no understanding of the job market, or of what is required to secure a job offer. For these people their job search will be a hit-and-miss affair, often full of disappointment. But take heart – the purpose of this book is to provide you with the professional support you will need to succeed in the job market.

The first part of this book provides support for those who have found themselves in the job market because of redundancy by helping to put the feelings you may experience into perspective. However, Chapters 4 and 5 should be read by everyone, since they focus on the importance of self-assessment and the understanding of your skills and strengths as part

*Introduction*

of the job-search process. Part Two of this book features job search topics which are wide-ranging so that every possible method for securing a new job is explored and evaluated.

> *'Nothing we ever imagined is beyond our powers,
> only beyond our present self-knowledge'*
> Theodore Roszak

# 2

# The Importance of Positive Thinking

*'Nothing great was ever achieved without enthusiasm'*
Ralph Waldo Emerson

There is a great deal to be said for the power of positive thinking and nowhere is this more important than in the field of job search. Optimism can help you to be happier, healthier and more successful. Pessimism leads, by contrast, to hopelessness and failure and is linked to depression, loneliness and painful shyness. Your abilities do count, but the belief that you *can* succeed affects whether or not you *will*.

Optimism and taking a positive approach to your job search helps to keep you in control. If a pessimist fails to secure interviews he will say to himself 'I'm not good enough' or 'I never seem to get anywhere'. Pessimism is all about blaming yourself when things go wrong, assuming fate has dealt you another blow. Negative thoughts spell gloom and doom, they sabotage confidence instead of offering support and encouragement, so you don't seek advice because you assume nothing can be done. The optimist will look for other reasons and will bounce back with a fresh approach; is much more inclined to act quickly, look for solutions, form a plan for action and reach out for advice. When things do go right, the optimist will take credit while the pessimist sees success as a fluke.

Pessimism is a hard habit to break – but it can be done.

Positive thinking leads to positive action – and reaction – so setting out to take full control when you're looking for a job is essential.

It is equally important that you have confidence in your own personal worth. If you have a poor self-image you are much more likely to have negative attitudes, and therefore to encounter failure.

Constantly comparing yourself with someone else who may be better qualified or superior in skill can diminish your sense of self-worth. For example, telling yourself 'I'm just a sales representative' or 'I've only got three O-levels' will destroy your self-confidence.

As with positive thinking, you can change your self-perception. You are who you are, so set out to make the most of your individuality.

Begin by focusing on your strengths and not your weaknesses – in other words accentuating the positive. Give yourself credit for your achievements and the skills and experience you have acquired. This should boost your motivation and improve your self-confidence. Next, picture yourself full of confidence and succeeding. This is not as silly as it may sound. Constantly imprinting this picture on your subconscious will affect your attitude to life; you should begin to feel more confident with a strong desire and expectation to succeed.

Negative thoughts will hold you back, so why not change them? When things go wrong, write down your negative thoughts – this can help to bring things out into the open and often acts as an emotional safety valve. Tell yourself you can dispel these thoughts by reacting differently and focusing on positive action and reaction. Of course there are no guarantees, but by giving yourself a chance you have everything to gain.

There are obviously going to be times when a confident

attitude is difficult to sustain. Recruitment is a very competitive business and the employer holds most of the cards. There are going to be times when you know you gave the best interview of your life but the employer sends you a short impersonal letter informing you that they have offered the post to a more suitable applicant; or a search and selection consultant contacts you to discuss a job you feel particularly well qualified for and you wait several weeks, only to be informed that the employer no longer wishes to fill the job.

To succeed, you must know how to handle rejection and bounce back. Of course it helps to know what may have let you down, and some employers and consultants are particularly helpful in providing invaluable feedback, but it is important not to dwell on this for too long. Think of it as a learning experience and tell yourself you won't make the same mistake again. Remember to maintain the picture of yourself full of confidence and succeeding.

Before you can get to where you want to be in terms of your job search and career, you need to have goals or objectives. These enable you to focus your will to move in the right direction. Set goals by writing them down and then commit yourself to achieving them. Continually review your list of goals and if you decide one should be adjusted or replaced with a better one, make amendments. Remember, it is important to bring into the picture not only what you can do but also what you *want* to do. Think about what you like and dislike in your current work: your preferences in the type of work you do, how you work, and the context in which you work.

Finally, it is worth repeating that positive thinking leads to positive action – and reaction. What you expect from your efforts, the evidence suggests, is what you're likely to get.

"I ALWAYS BORROW FROM YOU BECAUSE YOU'RE A PESSIMIST - YOU NEVER EXPECT IT BACK ANYWAY!"

# 3

# Redundancy – Facing Up To The Future

*'Man can be as big as he wants. No problem of human destiny is beyond human beings'*
John F. Kennedy

## What is Redundancy?

If you find yourself unemployed but with an extended period of notice, in receipt of a golden handshake or if you are dismissed with only a few hours' notice, it may amount to the same thing – your employer has terminated your employment by reason of redundancy.

Sometimes the word *redundant* is used to cover the general state of being unemployed. However The Employment Protection (Consolidation) Act 1978 defines redundancy as arising where:

(a) the employer ceases to carry on the business in which the employee was engaged – or closes the place in which the employee was working;
(b) the business ceases to require people with the particular skills of the employee or needs fewer of them to carry out the work.

Remember, employers can apply quite a wide interpretation to this definition, since the reason why they require fewer employees does not affect the employee's right to be considered as redundant.

## The Feelings you Encounter

When the term 'unemployment' first appeared in the *Encyclopaedia Britannica* in 1911, it was described as 'a condition of being unemployed amongst the working classes'. Clearly this is no longer the case, with unemployment increasingly affecting people whether they are at the top or the bottom of their chosen profession, in all types of businesses and organisations.

Whilst redundancy is much more common today amongst all kinds of workers, the stigma of redundancy is still difficult for many to bear. However, is it really a stigma any longer? My own view is that those in the business of selecting people for jobs no longer view redundancy as something to be ashamed of. They accept it for what it is; something that affects a large part of the working population – not just because of a downturn in the economy, but because of the rate of technological change and other factors.

If change is being forced on you through redundancy, then looking for a job can often be traumatic. It can be threatening, worrisome, and one of the testing times in life which ranks very highly as a personal stress experience. For many, redundancy is experienced as rejection, and rejection cuts into our sense of self-worth.

People do vary in temperament, but there are two views of redundancy which seem to predominate. The first is that redundancy is like bereavement; akin to the loss of a close member of the family. The second view reveals the value which society has made us place on our work. To lose one's job is to lose one's self-respect and to feel ashamed.

If you have lost your job because of redundancy, it is important for you to take responsibility for your situation and your feelings about it. When people recover from the initial shock of redundancy, they may feel optimistic about securing another job and have the situation under control. However, the most important point is to maintain a high degree of optimism throughout your job search and to face any unpleasant emotions head-on. It is worth recognising that there are already enough difficulties in carrying out your search for a job, without adding others because of an inability to face up to the reality of your emotions and feelings. Remember, unresolved feelings can seriously stand in the way of rational decision-making.

You may feel anger and resentment and believe that you have been treated badly – there's nothing wrong with this as long as you allow these feelings to come to the surface. To survive, you must rise above these emotions and feelings. Look toward the future, not backward toward the past. Staying rooted in your anger will not only sap up a lot of energy that you need to utilise to face the future but may also wreck your life. One way out is to find a relative or close friend, someone you can rely on to be honest, who can offer you support together with constructive criticism.

Redundancy can also bring depression – constituted of feelings such as sadness, dejection, apathy or generally being at a low point, particularly when unemployment stretches on. Financial worries often contribute to these feelings of helplessness. To avoid depression it is important to follow the advice about maintaining a positive attitude in Chapter 2, and you will find several other strategies well worth considering later in this chapter.

## Making the Best of a Difficult Situation

If you have only recently been given notice of redundancy, you may already be experiencing some of the unpleasant feelings mentioned above, particularly those of anger and resentment toward your employer. You may even be thinking of 'burning your boats', so to speak, and telling your boss exactly what you think of him and the company. However, despite the boost to your ego and the short-term feeling of satisfaction this may give you, you would be best advised to dismiss it entirely from your mind.

If you vent your anger on your employer, you will lose their goodwill. It is bound to affect their overall opinion of you and may lead to a less than beneficial comment being passed to any prospective employer seeking a reference. Instead, try to leave your employer with dignity, retaining their goodwill. This approach does have its benefits; for example, if you need time off from work to attend interviews or to carry out research, you will find your employer much more co-operative if you have kept your relationship on an even keel.

If your employer has not offered you the kind of help you think you might need, then don't be afraid to put together a list of what you require and to ask for their assistance. Even if they don't meet all your requirements, you may be pleasantly surprised with the help they do offer. Most employers would like to think they had given you some support in securing a new job. Even for those employers who find the subject of redundancy embarrassing, bringing it out into the open in this way will often enable them to see the positive side of supporting their staff during a difficult time. One major plus for a helpful employer is that the morale amongst the staff not affected by redundancy is often improved if they can see help and guidance being given to their less fortunate colleagues.

## Rights of Redundant Employees

If you are being made redundant, you must claim all that you are entitled to by legislation and your contract of employment. To begin with, find your 'written particulars of terms of employment', staff handbook and any other contractual paperwork. These documents should contain details of the period of notice to which you are entitled, how your redundancy payment is calculated, your entitlement under the pension scheme rules and how outstanding holiday entitlement is dealt with. Your employer should have provided you with written notice of redundancy which should explain your position with regard to each one of these terms. Once you have the letter you can compare this with your entitlement under your employment contract to satisfy yourself that your employer has met all his obligations.

### Your Statutory Rights

It is important that you understand your rights under current employment legislation when you are made redundant. Known as Statutory Rights they are as follows:

(a) Provided you have two or more years' service after the age of 18 with your employer you are entitled to redundancy pay;
(b) You have the right to receive your statutory or contractual period of notice from your employer;
(c) You have the right to paid time off work to look for another job or to arrange training.

## How to calculate your redundancy payment

The amount of redundancy pay to which you are entitled will depend upon your contract of employment, any trade union agreement which has been made, and on the current limits of State redundancy payments. Many employers offer redundancy terms which are more generous than those which are laid down by the State, and trade union agreements may also make provision for substantial payments.

In the absence of any specific redundancy terms offered by your employer then your employer must comply with the current limits of State redundancy payments. The size of a State redundancy payment will depend on your length of service, your age and a week's pay as defined in the Employment Protection (Consolidation) Act. Legislation sets out the maximum amount for a week's pay and this figure is reviewed annually. If, after calculating your actual week's pay, it is less than the statutory maximum currently in force then your actual pay will be used to determine your State redundancy payment. If your actual week's pay should exceed the statutory maximum currently in force, the statutory maximum will be used as the calculator for a week's pay.

You must have two years' service with your current employer to be entitled to any payment whatsoever for redundancy. The maximum service which can be taken into account is 20 years, and the greatest amount of redundancy pay which is payable is 30 weeks. For calculation purposes, only whole years of service are counted.

State redundancy payments are calculated by multiplying a week's pay (or ½ or 1½ times a week's pay, depending on age in each year of service) by the number of complete years of service as follows:

(a) for each complete year of employment in which the employee was not below the age of 41 but was below the age of 65 – *one and a half weeks' pay;*
(b) for each complete year of employment in which the employee was not below the age of 22 but was below the age of 41 – *one week's pay;*
(c) for each complete year of employment in which the employee was not below the age of 18 but was below the age of 22 – *half a week's pay.*
(d) Service with an employer whilst under the age of 18 does not count, nor does service over the normal retirement age.

## *Employees nearing pensionable age*

If you are within 12 months of your 65th birthday, you will have your statutory redundancy entitlement reduced by one-twelfth in respect of each month you remain in employment after attaining the age of 64. This means in effect, that if you are made redundant very close to the age of 65, the amount of compensation you would receive is minimal (see example 3 later in this chapter).

## *Calculating the number of weeks' pay*

The ready reckoner table on the following page can be used to calculate the precise number of weeks' pay to which you are entitled. Some examples of redundancy payment calculations have also been included.

## Manage Your Career

# Redundancy Payment Table*

The following ready reckoner table will enable you to calculate the precise number of weeks' pay to which you are entitled. To use the table, read off your age and number of completed years' service. The table will then show how many weeks' pay you are entitled to. The table starts at 20 because no one below this age can qualify for a redundancy payment and service before the age of 18 does not count. For women and men aged between 64 and 65, the cash amount due is reduced by one-twelfth for every complete month by which the age exceeds 64.

| Service (years) | 2 | 3 | 4 | 5 | 6 | 7 | 8 | 9 | 10 | 11 | 12 | 13 | 14 | 15 | 16 | 17 | 18 | 19 | 20 |
|---|---|---|---|---|---|---|---|---|---|---|---|---|---|---|---|---|---|---|---|
| age (years) | | | | | | | | | | | | | | | | | | | |
| 20 | 1 | 1 | 1 | 1 | - | | | | | | | | | | | | | | |
| 21 | 1 | 1½ | 1½ | 1½ | 1½ | - | | | | | | | | | | | | | |
| 22 | 1 | 1½ | 2 | 2 | 2 | 2 | - | | | | | | | | | | | | |
| 23 | 1½ | 2 | 2½ | 3 | 3 | 3 | 3 | - | | | | | | | | | | | |
| 24 | 2 | 2½ | 3 | 3½ | 4 | 4 | 4 | 4 | - | | | | | | | | | | |
| 25 | 2 | 3 | 3½ | 4 | 4½ | 5 | 5 | 5 | 5 | - | | | | | | | | | |
| 26 | 2 | 3 | 4 | 4½ | 5 | 5½ | 6 | 6 | 6 | 6 | - | | | | | | | | |
| 27 | 2 | 3 | 4 | 5 | 5½ | 6 | 6½ | 7 | 7 | 7 | 7 | - | | | | | | | |
| 28 | 2 | 3 | 4 | 5 | 6 | 6½ | 7 | 7½ | 8 | 8 | 8 | 8 | - | | | | | | |
| 29 | 2 | 3 | 4 | 5 | 6 | 7 | 7½ | 8 | 8½ | 9 | 9 | 9 | 9 | - | | | | | |
| 30 | 2 | 3 | 4 | 5 | 6 | 7 | 8 | 8½ | 9 | 9½ | 10 | 10 | 10 | 10 | - | | | | |
| 31 | 3 | 4 | 5 | 6 | 7 | 8 | 9 | 9½ | 10 | 10½ | 11 | 11 | 11 | 11 | - | | | | |
| 32 | 2 | 3 | 4 | 5 | 6 | 7 | 8 | 9 | 10 | 10½ | 11 | 11½ | 12 | 12 | 12 | - | | | |
| 33 | 2 | 3 | 4 | 5 | 6 | 7 | 8 | 9 | 10 | 11 | 11½ | 12 | 12½ | 13 | 13 | 13 | - | | |
| 34 | 2 | 3 | 4 | 5 | 6 | 7 | 8 | 9 | 10 | 11 | 12 | 12½ | 13 | 13½ | 14 | 14 | 14 | - | |
| 35 | 2 | 3 | 4 | 5 | 6 | 7 | 8 | 9 | 10 | 11 | 12 | 13 | 13½ | 14 | 14½ | 15 | 15 | 15 | 15 |
| 36 | 2 | 3 | 4 | 5 | 6 | 7 | 8 | 9 | 10 | 11 | 12 | 13 | 14 | 14½ | 15 | 15½ | 16 | 16 | 16 |
| 37 | 2 | 3 | 4 | 5 | 6 | 7 | 8 | 9 | 10 | 11 | 12 | 13 | 14 | 15 | 15½ | 16 | 16½ | 17 | 17 |
| 38 | 2 | 3 | 4 | 5 | 6 | 7 | 8 | 9 | 10 | 11 | 12 | 13 | 14 | 15 | 16 | 16½ | 17 | 17½ | 18 |
| 39 | 2 | 3 | 4 | 5 | 6 | 7 | 8 | 9 | 10 | 11 | 12 | 13 | 14 | 15 | 16 | 17 | 17½ | 18 | 18½ |
| 40 | 2 | 3 | 4 | 5 | 6 | 7 | 8 | 9 | 10 | 11 | 12 | 13 | 14 | 15 | 16 | 17 | 18 | 18½ | 19 |
| 41 | 2 | 3 | 4 | 5 | 6 | 7 | 8 | 9 | 10 | 11 | 12 | 13 | 14 | 15 | 16 | 17 | 18 | 19 | 19½ |
| 42 | 2½ | 3½ | 4½ | 5½ | 6½ | 7½ | 8½ | 9½ | 10½ | 11½ | 12½ | 13½ | 14½ | 15½ | 16½ | 17½ | 18½ | 19½ | 20½ |
| 43 | 3 | 4 | 5 | 6 | 7 | 8 | 9 | 10 | 11 | 12 | 13 | 14 | 15 | 16 | 17 | 18 | 19 | 20 | 21 |
| 44 | 3 | 4½ | 5½ | 6½ | 7½ | 8½ | 9½ | 10½ | 11½ | 12½ | 13½ | 14½ | 15½ | 16½ | 17½ | 18½ | 19½ | 20½ | 21½ |
| 45 | 3 | 4½ | 6 | 7 | 8 | 9 | 10 | 11 | 12 | 13 | 14 | 15 | 16 | 17 | 18 | 19 | 20 | 21 | 22 |
| 46 | 3 | 4½ | 6 | 7½ | 8½ | 9½ | 10½ | 11½ | 12½ | 13½ | 14½ | 15½ | 16½ | 17½ | 18½ | 19½ | 20½ | 21½ | 22½ |
| 47 | 3 | 4½ | 6 | 7½ | 9 | 10 | 11 | 12 | 13 | 14 | 15 | 16 | 17 | 18 | 19 | 20 | 21 | 22 | 23 |
| 48 | 3 | 4½ | 6 | 7½ | 9 | 10½ | 11½ | 12½ | 13½ | 14½ | 15½ | 16½ | 17½ | 18½ | 19½ | 20½ | 21½ | 22½ | 23½ |
| 49 | 3 | 4½ | 6 | 7½ | 9 | 10½ | 12 | 13 | 14 | 15 | 16 | 17 | 18 | 19 | 20 | 21 | 22 | 23 | 24 |

| Age | | | | | | | | | | | | | | | | | | | | | | |
|---|---|---|---|---|---|---|---|---|---|---|---|---|---|---|---|---|---|---|---|---|---|---|
| 50 | 3 | 4½ | 6 | 7½ | 9 | 10½ | 12 | 13½ | 14½ | 15½ | 16½ | 17½ | 18½ | 19½ | 20½ | 21½ | 22½ | 23½ | 24½ | | | |
| 51 | 3 | 4½ | 6 | 7½ | 9 | 10½ | 12 | 13½ | 15 | 16 | 17 | 18 | 19 | 20 | 21 | 22 | 23 | 24 | 25 | | | |
| 52 | 3 | 4½ | 6 | 7½ | 9 | 10½ | 12 | 13½ | 15 | 16½ | 17½ | 18½ | 19½ | 20½ | 21½ | 22½ | 23½ | 24½ | 25½ | | | |
| 53 | 3 | 4½ | 6 | 7½ | 9 | 10½ | 12 | 13½ | 15 | 16½ | 18 | 19 | 20 | 21 | 22 | 23 | 24 | 25 | 26 | | | |
| 54 | 3 | 4½ | 6 | 7½ | 9 | 10½ | 12 | 13½ | 15 | 16½ | 18 | 19½ | 20½ | 21½ | 22½ | 23½ | 24½ | 25½ | 26½ | | | |
| 55 | 3 | 4½ | 6 | 7½ | 9 | 10½ | 12 | 13½ | 15 | 16½ | 18 | 19½ | 21 | 22 | 23 | 24 | 25 | 26 | 27 | | | |
| 56 | 3 | 4½ | 6 | 7½ | 9 | 10½ | 12 | 13½ | 15 | 16½ | 18 | 19½ | 21 | 22½ | 23½ | 24½ | 25½ | 26½ | 27½ | | | |
| 57 | 3 | 4½ | 6 | 7½ | 9 | 10½ | 12 | 13½ | 15 | 16½ | 18 | 19½ | 21 | 22½ | 24 | 25 | 26 | 27 | 28 | | | |
| 58 | 3 | 4½ | 6 | 7½ | 9 | 10½ | 12 | 13½ | 15 | 16½ | 18 | 19½ | 21 | 22½ | 24 | 25½ | 26½ | 27½ | 28½ | | | |
| 59 | 3 | 4½ | 6 | 7½ | 9 | 10½ | 12 | 13½ | 15 | 16½ | 18 | 19½ | 21 | 22½ | 24 | 25½ | 27 | 28 | 29 | | | |
| 60 | 3 | 4½ | 6 | 7½ | 9 | 10½ | 12 | 13½ | 15 | 16½ | 18 | 19½ | 21 | 22½ | 24 | 25½ | 27 | 28½ | 29½ | | | |
| 61 | 3 | 4½ | 6 | 7½ | 9 | 10½ | 12 | 13½ | 15 | 16½ | 18 | 19½ | 21 | 22½ | 24 | 25½ | 27 | 28½ | 30 | | | |
| 62 | 3 | 4½ | 6 | 7½ | 9 | 10½ | 12 | 13½ | 15 | 16½ | 18 | 19½ | 21 | 22½ | 24 | 25½ | 27 | 28½ | 30 | | | |
| 63 | 3 | 4½ | 6 | 7½ | 9 | 10½ | 12 | 13½ | 15 | 16½ | 18 | 19½ | 21 | 22½ | 24 | 25½ | 27 | 28½ | 30 | | | |
| 64 | 3 | 4½ | 6 | 7½ | 9 | 10½ | 12 | 13½ | 15 | 16½ | 18 | 19½ | 21 | 22½ | 24 | 25½ | 27 | 28½ | 30 | | | |

*Source: DTI Publication 'Redundancy Payments' Ref: PL 808 (REV 3)

The following examples will help you to understand how State redundancy payments are calculated.

*Example 1*

David is 45 years of age, his date of birth is 6 April 1952 and he has been employed by his company since 1 June 1985. He works full-time and is earning £26,800 per annum which is £515.38 per week. He is made redundant on 30 September 1997 and has therefore been employed by the company for twelve years and four months.

His statutory redundancy entitlement is 14 weeks at the statutory maximum currently in force.

This is based on:

(a) one and a half week's pay for each complete year of employment in which the employee was not below the age of 41 but was below the age of 65, i.e. 4 × 1½ = 6 (part-years of service do not count).

(b) one week's pay for each complete year of employment in which the employee was not below the age of 22 but was below the age of 41, i.e. 8 × 1 = 8
(c) David's actual weekly pay is higher than the statutory maximum currently in force so the statutory maximum is used as the calculator for a week's pay.

*Example 2*

Jean is 31 years of age, her date of birth is 8 October 1965 and commenced employment with the company when aged 17 on 1 December 1982. She works full-time and is earning £10,400 per annum which is £200 per week. She is made redundant on 30 May 1997 and has therefore been employed by the company for fourteen years and six months.

Her statutory redundancy entitlement is 11 weeks at £200 = £2,200.

This is based on:

(a) one week's pay for each complete year of employment in which the employee was not below the age of 22 but was below the age of 41, i.e. 9 × 1 = 9 (part-years of service do not count).
(b) half a week's pay for each complete year of employment in which the employee was not below the age of 18 but was below the age of 22, i.e. 4 × ½ = 2
(c) Her service before the age of 18 because service below that does not count.
(d) Jean's actual weekly pay is used for calculation purposes because it is lower than the statutory maximum currently in force.

## Example 3

Robert is 64 years of age, his date of birth is 30 October 1932 and he has been employed by his company since 1 February 1979. He works full-time and is earning £10,140 per annum which is £195.00 per week. He is made redundant on 13 June 1997 and has therefore been employed by the company for eighteen years and seven months.

His statutory redundancy entitlement is £2,193.75.

This is based on

(a) one and a half week's pay for each complete year of employment in which the employee was not below the age of 41 but was below the age of 65, i.e. 18 × 1½ = 27 (part-years of service do not count).

(d) Robert's actual weekly pay is used for calculation purposes because it is lower than the statutory maximum currently in force.

$$27 \times £195.00 = £5,265.00.$$

However, because at the date of his redundancy, Robert is already over 64 years of age and would have retired at age 65, his entitlement is reduced by $1/12$ for every month over the age of 64, in his case, seven months at the time of redundancy. His £5,265 therefore is reduced by $7/12$ and he would receive £2,193.75.

## Example 4

Mary is 25 years of age, her date of birth is 7 August 1971 and she commenced employment with the company on 10 April 1992. She works full-time and is earning £16,250 per annum which is £312.50 per week. She is made redundant on 15 May 1997 and has therefore been employed by the company for five years and one month.

Her statutory redundancy entitlement is 4 weeks at the statutory maximum currently in force.

This is based on:

(a) one week's pay for each complete year of employment in which the employee was not below the age of 22 but was below the age of 41, i.e. $3 \times 1 = 3$ (part-years of service do not count)
(b) half a week's pay for each complete year of employment in which the employee was not below the age of 18 but was below the age of 22, i.e. $2 \times \frac{1}{2} = 1$
(c) Mary's actual weekly pay is higher than the statutory maximum currently in force so the statutory maximum is used as the calculator for a week's pay.

As the statutory limit of a week's pay for redundancy purposes is normally reviewed on an annual basis, you would be wise to establish the current value with the Department of Employment. The Redundancy Payments Service of the Department of Employment has a free helpline which is manned from 9am-5pm Monday to Friday and the number is 0800 848489. The service is designed mainly for people who need help because their employer has gone out of business or cannot afford to make the statutory payments. Information and advice is also give on particular problems such as checking on the progress of a claim and making complaints. You can obtain a leaflet, *Redundancy Payments Service Charter: How We Can Help* from your local Jobcentre or by ringing the helpline.

## Notice

Anyone who is made redundant is entitled to their statutory or contractual period of notice. To establish this check out your 'written particulars of terms of employment', staff handbook and any other contractual paperwork.

In the absence of any special terms agreed with your employer, then the following statutory periods of notice will apply:

| Service with your employer | Notice entitlement |
|---|---|
| one month or more but less than two years: | one week |
| two years or more but less than 12 years: | one week for each year of continuous employment |
| 12 years or more: | not less than 12 weeks |

If you are a member of an independent recognised trade union, your period of notice must also take account of the requirement for your employer to consult with the trade union in advance of the redundancies. If you have any concerns about this requirement, your trade union official should be able to help.

## Problems you might encounter in obtaining redundancy compensation

If the company you have worked for is insolvent it will be unable to pay you your redundancy payment. In these circumstances, your employer should provide you with a form supplied by the Department of Employment for you to claim this compensation. If your employer doesn't comply with this procedure you should contact your local Jobcentre or use the free helpline number mentioned earlier. The Department of Employment will wish to satisfy itself that your employer is insolvent and has received a statement from the Receiver, Liquidator or Trustee that you are entitled to the debt claimed.

If your employer has not paid you redundancy compensation for a reason other than insolvency, then you must show your intention to claim by lodging with your employer a letter stating that you were dismissed by reason of redundancy and that you are entitled to claim a redundancy payment. Be sure to keep a copy of this letter for your own records. This letter must be lodged with your employer within six months of the relevant date of dismissal – this is the date when your notice expires, or earlier if you were paid salary in lieu of notice. If, after receiving your letter, your employer still refuses to pay you redundancy compensation, then you can make a complaint to an industrial tribunal. Your local Jobcentre will supply you with the appropriate forms for completion and referral to the industrial tribunal.

## *Redundancy pay, salary in lieu of notice and tax*

Redundancy pay is free of tax up to the Inland Revenue current limit of £30,000. Any amount of your redundancy payment over this limit will be taxed at your normal rate of tax. However, if you should receive any payments which are not solely on account of your redundancy as defined by the Employment Protection (Consolidation) Act and explained earlier in this chapter, they may be subject to tax in full. For example, these would include payments which are a form of terminal bonus.

If your employer should offer you the services of an outplacement company, the cost or value of this service is not taxable, even when it brings the total value of the redundancy payment over the £30,000 threshold.

You may be offered the choice of working out your notice or receiving a payment in lieu of notice. What are the pros and cons of either choice? You might be tempted to settle for payment in lieu of notice because this will leave you completely free to look for another job.

The Inland Revenue states that if a period of notice is written into your contract then any payments made under that provision are regarded as income and taxed accordingly; in other words the payment has to be one that you would not normally expect to receive. So, if such a payment is an ex gratia payment relating to the loss of your job, your payment may be free of tax, but then only if the total of your redundancy payment plus the ex gratia payment does not exceed the limit imposed by the Inland Revenue. Of course, if you carry on working you will be taxed at your normal rate.

Whilst your payment in lieu of notice may have tax benefits; you must bear in mind that receiving several months' salary in this way could well prejudice your entitlement to Job Seeker's Allowance for the same period. Even if the payment is described as ex gratia, the unemployment benefit adjudicating officer may decide that part or all of the payment was salary in lieu of notice and reduce your entitlement to unemployment benefit. If you disagree with this ruling there is an appeal process.

It is important to recognise that such payments can reduce very quickly if you take several months to find a job and you are still paying a mortgage, running a car and paying day-to-day household expenses.

Finally, a point worth remembering is that it is often said that you will find it easier to secure another job if you are still employed and actually work out your period of notice.

## Time off to look for work or to arrange training

Whilst legislation does not lay down any specific amount of time off to which you are entitled in a redundancy situation, industrial tribunal cases have indicated that a maximum of two days per week would not be unreasonable.

## Taking Care of Yourself

Whilst you're looking for a job your physical well-being is very important. There are a number of simple rules to follow such as making sure you get enough regular exercise – a daily walk is a good idea for getting out in the open air or a visit to your local swimming baths several times a week. Eat healthy, well-balanced meals. Reserve your sleep only for night time. If you are tempted to sleep during the day, you can be sure this will have a detrimental effect when you lie awake all night with your mind building and rebuilding the channel tunnel!

Structure a daily routine that includes time for your job search, time with your family and time for yourself, whether this be keeping fit or a personal hobby or interest.

## Personal Finance

### A Personal Balance Sheet

If you are faced with the prospect of redundancy, financial worries are inevitable. The sooner you draw up a personal balance sheet or a statement of your financial situation, the better. One side of the balance sheet should represent your current outgoings and the other side should represent your sources of income. If you find a new job on similar terms and conditions to your old job in a matter of only a few weeks, then you may be able to set aside the balance sheet. On the other hand, as the odds suggest that it will take much longer to secure another job, then the need for a personal balance sheet is more than justified.

If you have received a sizeable redundancy payment you may be tempted to splash out on a holiday or new furniture and carpet for the house. My advice is – however tempting – don't! You will need to make this money last until you can secure another job. During a period of unemployment, you will still have to pay your mortgage, the usual gas and electricity bills as well as the cost of your weekly visit to the supermarket.

Now, more than ever, you need sound, expert, independent advice. If you already have a financial advisor, that's fine. If not, and if your financial affairs are fairly straightforward, you should be able to obtain the help you need from your bank manager or accountant. However if your financial affairs are more complex, you may need help from a tax-planning expert or independent financial advisor. Whichever route you take – remember to budget for their fee!

## Mortgage

If you have a mortgage you must consult your lender, explain that you have lost your job through redundancy and try to negotiate an amount of repayment with which you can manage.

## Pension arrangements

What should you do about your pension? This may seem a complex topic, but if you have worked for a company providing their own pension scheme, then the options are really straightforward. If you have worked for your employer for less than two years, you may be able to obtain a refund of your contributions; you could freeze your pension and leave it with your last employer; you could transfer your pension into a new employer's scheme; you could transfer the fund or value of your pension into an insurance company pension scheme and finally, if you are eligible, you could take early retirement and an immediate pension. Your choice will depend upon the rules of your employer's scheme and a range of other personal factors, all of which must be taken into account. Clearly it would be unwise to expand further on this subject because you really need to take expert advice from a pensions consultant. If you would like the names and addresses of local pensions consultants these can be obtained from: The Society of Pensions Consultants, Ludgate House, Ludgate Circus, London EC4A 2AB. Telephone 0171 353 1688.

## Investments
You will also need specialist advice if you have money invested. Your professionally qualified accountant may be acting as your investment adviser, otherwise ensure that your adviser is licensed by FIMBRA – The Financial Intermediaries, Managers and Brokers Regulatory Association, and be sure to ask what commission they receive if you invest as they advise.

## Income Tax
Contact your local tax office to find out if and when you can expect to receive a tax rebate. However the Inland Revenue are not renowned for their speed, and consequently it is more likely that you will have to wait until the end of the tax year or when you return to employment before such a rebate will be made.

If your tax affairs are complex, you may feel that it would be of benefit to employ a professionally qualified accountant to provide you with advice and to help complete the tax return for you. Be sure to ask for an estimate of his fees before handing over your files.

## Private Health Insurance Schemes

If your previous employer provided you with a group health insurance scheme, it is possible to convert this into an individual plan with the same insurer. There are benefits in that most insurers will disregard any previous claims history at the time of transfer, but unfortunately you can expect a hefty increase in the rate of premium. Before signing up with your current insurer you would be wise to shop around and check out the premiums and benefits with alternative insurers

## State Benefits

If you are entitled to State benefits set aside any misguided feelings of pride and take full advantage of these benefits – they can often keep your balance sheet in credit. Visit your local Jobcentre and Benefits Agency to check out your entitlement to Jobseeker's Allowance (JSA), Family Credit, Housing Benefit and Council Tax Benefit etc., but don't wait! Very few of these benefits can be paid retrospectively. Leaflets on all these benefits are available from your local Jobcentre or Benefits Agency.

If you are unemployed, you may now be eligible to claim Jobseeker's Allowance (JSA) by applying at your local Jobcentre. Contributory JSA replaced Unemployment Benefit and Means-tested JSA replaced Income Support in October 1996. To qualify for Jobseeker's Allowance you must be out of work, or working less than 16 hours a week, but actively seeking work, of course. You will need to agree and sign a Jobseeker's Agreement and have paid enough National Insurance Contributions, or have income and savings below a certain level.

The Jobseeker's Agreement is a written agreement between you and an Employment Service Adviser about how you will try to get back to work. The Agreement sets out the types of jobs and hours you are willing to do, what you are going to do to find work, how the Jobcentre will help and how you and the Employment Service Adviser will review your progress. Your progress will be reviewed at fortnightly meetings with the Employment Service Adviser, and provided this review is satisfactory, the Adviser will trigger a JSA payment.

As I mentioned earlier, Contributory JSA replaced unemployment benefit and can be payable for a maximum of 26 weeks (182 days). It is not a means-tested benefit but is based on your National Insurance Contributions. To qualify, you must have paid or been credited with sufficient Class 1 National Insurance Contributions during two relevant tax years. This means that only those who have worked for someone else (not the self-employed) will be eligible since they are the only group who pay Class 1 contributions.

You can be disqualified from receiving Contributory JSA for a minimum of one week (7 days) and a maximum of 26 weeks if you left your job voluntarily without a good reason, or if your employer dismissed you for misconduct. In both cases, you and your employer will be asked to say why the employment ended. A similar period of disqualification applies if you fail to apply for a job vacancy or neglect to take up a reasonable opportunity for employment. People can also be disqualified for two weeks if they refuse to comply with the direction of their Employment Service Adviser if this was reasonable in their case. None of these benefit penalties can be imposed until an Adjudicating Officer has made a decision.

You may be eligible for Means-tested JSA if your payment of Contributory JSA is delayed or if you are not entitled to Contributory JSA. Whether you are entitled to Means-tested JSA will depend upon your income from other sources, the income of other members of your family and the size of your savings, property, insurance policies and whether you are receiving any other benefits. They will also take into account claims for dependants and certain regular outgoings such as the cost of your mortgage etc.

If you have worked out your period of notice, you should either call into your local Jobcentre or telephone to make an appointment. If you have not worked your period of notice, but have been paid salary in lieu of notice, you should still make an appointment, but you will not be entitled to receive any Jobseeker's Allowance until the period which this sum of money covers has lapsed. In any event you will not receive any money for the first three days of your claim, which are called waiting days. If you do not make an appointment on the first day of your unemployment, you may lose money, because payment cannot usually be backdated. The Jobcentre will need to know your National Insurance Number as soon as possible and you should also give them your P45 tax form.

One further important reason for registering with the Jobcentre, even if there is doubt about your entitlement to benefit, is that you will receive National Insurance credits. This will prevent problems affecting your entitlement to other benefits such as Retirement Pension, at a later date.

If you are not entitled to Contributory JSA, you will be informed in writing. If you do not agree with the decision, you can appeal against it to a Social Security Appeal Tribunal. The Jobcentre will tell you about this process.

If you have been entitled to JSA for over 91 days you may be able to build up a *Back to Work Bonus* from any part-time work or part-time self employed work. The bonus amount will be equal to half your earnings above any disregarded amounts from any part-time work you undertake whilst claiming JSA. You may also be entitled to a maximum of £1,000 as a tax-free lump sum when you move into work which causes your entitlement to JSA to cease.

Coping with the frustrations and complexities of claiming Jobseeker's Allowance requires stamina, patience and a good sense of humour. Be prepared to complete what may seem like an endless supply of forms and to answer personal questions. To find the Jobcentre or Benefits Agency for your area look in your local telephone book. Try phoning them if you need more help and information on JSA and other Social Security benefits, or use the following numbers for which there is no charge:

  Freeline Social Security   –  0800 666 555
  Benefits Enquiry Line    –  0800 88 22 00

The operators who take your call on these freeline numbers do not have access to your personal records, but will be able to give you general advice.

## A Friend in Need

Getting support during your job search is very important. Of course, if you have access to someone who is professionally qualified in the field of career counselling this will be very helpful, but what you also need is support from your family and close friends. Being able to bounce your ideas off someone you can trust goes a long way to avoiding feelings of being out there on your own.

It is important that you come to terms with the experience of redundancy. You are not the first to find yourself in this position and you must set your strengths to finding a way through to the other side of these feelings. Once you can set these emotions to one side, you can channel all your energy into finding a new job.

Many people are totally unprepared for the impact on their morale when they find themselves in the job market. However, it can also be an exhilarating experience – a sense of the future opening up before you, an opportunity to take control, clear the decks and begin again.

# 4

# More of the Same? Or Time for a Change?

*'If you go to heaven without being naturally qualified for it, you will not enjoy yourself there'*
George Bernard Shaw

This is a very important question and consequently you must think carefully before giving an answer. Unless you are taking the first step on your personal career ladder you have an opportunity to change direction and even if you are seeking an improved position in the same field, there will still be a number of possible options for you to consider.

Many people, at some stage in their careers, despite experiencing some periods of stability and relative equilibrium in their lives and careers, want to change their type of job. The reasons vary for this, but quite often it has to do with:

- The need to make more money
- The desire to extend their source of knowledge and experience
- Failure to be promoted
- A change in family commitments
- The need to overcome boredom and frustration
- The need for a greater sense of self-value
- The desire to fulfil a long-cherished dream
- An external impetus, such as redundancy

People who are suffering from career problems of this kind notice others who appear happy, fulfilled and successful. These people may not necessarily be successful in the conventional career terms of having climbed the career ladder and achieved financial reward. Many are just as fulfilled and successful having decided to change the direction of their career completely. Such people may have moved laterally within a career path rather than upwards, or even moved away from a career altogether, seeing a job as a small and transitional part of their life. The one common link between these people is their decision to choose for themselves the direction they wish to take.

Whether you are starting out on a career, want to develop your current job, need to consider a career move, or are questioning your current work or job, you, too, have a choice. You can drift along and let chance determine your future, or you can begin to take charge of yourself and gain control over your destiny.

People are much more inclined to think about change today than, for example, they did in our parents' time. We are part of a generation enjoying considerably more freedom of choice. There are wider opportunities for higher education; people are better informed, have more cultural and leisure interests and many more people are home-owners. Our value in financial terms, our purchasing power and our quality of life are of a standard our parents could not begin to imagine.

## Self-assessment

So, if you have been thinking about a change, where do you begin? Well, there's a lot to consider, so try answering the following questions and decide what your answers say about you and the sort of job change you might make:

- What type of person are you?
- What are your views about life?
- How old are you?
- Are you married or single?
- If you are married do you have young children?
- Are your children at a critical age in terms of their education?
- What are your needs in financial terms?
- What is your degree of ambition?
- Does your health have any bearing on your choice of job?
- Would you prefer to work part-time?
- Do you want to move house?
- What is your degree of satisfaction with your current or last job?
- Do you need better job security?
- Would you prefer to be self-employed?
- Do you want a job involving less or more travel?
- Do you want to work indoors or outdoors?
- Do you want the prestige of working for a large organisation or a smaller company where you know everyone?
- Do you want an active/sedentary/artistic job etc?
- Do you want to work set hours or flexible working hours?
- Do you need freedom at weekends and in the evening?
- Do you want to work with young or older people, people with similar interests or lots of different people?
- Do you want to improve your education and qualifications?

Your personality and your general views on life will certainly affect whether you are happy enough to stay in a job in the same field or profession or whether you want to move on to something different. Redundancy often sparks people into trying something they have thought about for years. Trying something new involves risk, and when combined with several of the other factors in our list, may be enough to suggest that you stick with the familiar. However you may see this as just the opportunity you have been looking for, and risk may not be an issue if you feel sufficiently motivated enough to make a change. You can read more about the process of self-assessment in the next chapter.

## Are you in a rut?

For some people, their life is the same old routine. Every morning they get up and go to work, come home and read the paper, eat a meal, watch television and go to bed. Then they get up and go to work again. Some of these people no longer find their work interesting. Perhaps they have run out of promotion opportunities or their work is no longer challenging. Many ask themselves 'Am I really going to be doing this for the rest of my life?' Such people have 'plateaued' and feel trapped. They are often afraid and don't know how to break out of the rut, usually for one of the following reasons:

- They lack self-confidence
- They don't know where to start
- They don't know what is available
- They don't know if the risk is worth it
- They lack job-search skills
- They fear the prospect of failure
- They lack motivation
- They have had a bad experience when previously applying for a change of job

- They lack the skills required
- They put a high value on their current job security

When promotions do come to an end we sometimes feel a sense of failure or if we have fully mastered the work it can bring feelings of tedium. So what can we do to take us off this plateau?

If you have decided to wait for someone to notice you, you could be in for a long wait! You must create your own opportunities. Your responsibility is to take the talents you have – you know them better than anyone else – and ardently capitalise on them to gain the highest possible achievement. Don't be afraid to speak up and make a case for yourself.

Many of us find ourselves procrastinating from time to time and nowhere is this more evident than when we are faced with the prospect of a career change.

Those who procrastinate often assume that successful people achieve their goals without frustration, self-doubt and failure. This is unrealistic. Highly productive people know that life is frustrating. They assume they'll encounter obstacles; when they do, they persevere until they overcome them.

Every choice that you make will probably involve discarding many others. You may be anxious about choosing one way or the other when you reach major crossroads in your life because you want to keep all your options open. But the result is that you end up in a state of paralysis, failing to make any progress.

## Employment Trends

Trends in the employment market are changing with some industries contracting and others expanding. Entirely new jobs are being created, and others transform as technology develops. As a result, flexibility, maturity and the ability to learn new skills may be as valuable as actual experience in a particular field.

In many areas the skills a person started with are becoming outdated. The pattern and shape of the working day is altering. People either enhance their existing skills in mid-career and continue; or re-skill themselves and switch to something completely different. You may need to look at all the possibilities, including retraining, to develop your potential more fully and re-channel your efforts into new areas.

## Choosing a Job where Maturity is Valued

People are now healthier in their forties and fifties and feel they still have a long working life ahead of them. Many want to change career direction or discover they have unsuspected gifts and skills later in life. Often their children have left home, they've paid off most of the mortgage, and they can afford to take a chance.

While many employers still nurture prejudices against older people, some are becoming more receptive to the idea of taking on older people and experience is valued much more highly than it used to be.

The Open University offers a guide on the accessibility of different professions to older people. Teaching, health care, social work and office and retail management are listed among those ready to accept people regardless of age; advertising and journalism are among the hardest to crack.

In certain occupations, maturity is a positive advantage. Licensed retailers recruiting a pub manager, who may head a staff of fifty or more in a large pub, look neither for youth nor knowledge of the business. They usually prefer people with no previous experience in the licensing trade because they often have to undo bad habits during the training.

You're never too old to make a fresh start. Most people who are 'over the hill' are those who have *chosen* to be that way. Of course, it may be more difficult to learn skills that require specific physical strengths, but this is not so much of a deterrent as you may think, since there are schemes specifically designed for training the older worker.

You will discover that if you have the motivation to tackle something new and the determination to get something out of life, you can do it.

## *Examine your Finances*

If your career change involves an initial drop in income, as many do, think what it will mean. Can you afford to do without those little luxuries we sometimes take for granted? A student grant may be adequate for a 19-year-old, but for someone older it may mean a drastic change of lifestyle. Until you get established, running your own business could leave little cash for those luxuries that you previously took for granted.

You need to take a careful look at your lifestyle and examine all your financial commitments before embarking on any career change.

## *Involving your Partner*

It is important to involve your partner fully in the decision-making process, taking the financial insecurity of a change of career into account.

## Moving House

Are you prepared to move house if your new career requires it? What is the position with your current mortgage? Could you afford to increase your monthly mortgage repayments? These are a few of the financial considerations but there are also other factors to take into account such as the age of your children and whether a move at this time would disrupt their education. If you or your partner have ageing parents living in the same neighbourhood, how would you feel about moving away from them?

It is important that you research and assess the question of your mobility with particular care. If you have a family, you must take their needs into consideration. Discussions now will prevent you having to make pressurised decisions in the future. I can recall one job seeker from London who told me that it was only after having received a job offer to work in North Wales, that he discovered his wife did not consider moving that distance away an option for the family. He recognised that it was the lack of discussion, coupled with his eagerness to secure a suitable job which placed his marriage in jeopardy.

## Status

Concern for status is very important to some people, but if you have worked in a highly pressurised environment and are now unemployed, this is the ideal opportunity to reassess your working and personal life. Perhaps now is the time to step down the promotional ladder a rung or two in order to spend more time with your family.

## Salary and Benefits

Before you set out for more of the same or a change in your career, you need to research current salary trends for the job in question. Whilst we would all like to improve on our salary as we move from one employer to another, ask yourself what you would realistically anticipate and how flexible you could be. If you have to move, can your partner's job move also? If not, will your salary and benefits package be sufficient to compensate for the loss of that second income?

It is essential that you price yourself right in the market. If you are unemployed and had been with your last employer for a long period of time, then some of your salary was probably based on your experience of familiarity with that organisation. Is that familiarity worth anything to your next employer? The sheer numbers of excellent people seeking work has turned the job market into a buyers' market. You can no longer assume a salary increase when joining a new company, even if you have not received a salary increase in several years.

## Where can You use Your Skills?

You do need to consider the type of employer you would like to work for. Use the following list to help determine your preferences and when you have a list of your own rank them in order of importance to you:

- A company with 5 or fewer employees
- A company with 20 or fewer employees
- A company with 100 or fewer employees
- A company with 1000-plus employees
- Employment in a large city

- Employment in the suburbs
- Employment in the country
- A non-profit company or organisation
- A service organisation
- A well established company
- A recently formed company
- A company which is going places
- A company with a lot of problems

## Your Health

Your state of health will influence how you should handle the rest of your life. Just how healthy are you? How much stress can you tolerate? How much uncertainty? This is particularly important when you are planning to go into business on your own account, but you also need to think realistically about the hours you will need to work and about the stresses that the new line of work may impose. Are you fit to cope with them?

## Change to What?

You may have already decided what the change should be. However a career change is a momentous move so before you take any decision, make sure that you are really keen to tackle a new occupation, and not simply reacting to a temporary disappointment in your present career.

If you have not yet decided on your new career, here are some of the choices open to you:

- New employment
- Temporary employment and interim management

*More of the Same? Or Time for a Change?*

- Self-employment
- Voluntary work
- Further education

## New employment

A change of career is a major throw of the dice, but for those prepared to take the risk, it may be the best choice of all. However, you can improve your chances of obtaining employment if you apply for jobs in a growth area rather than one which is declining. The areas which are commonly thought to be expanding include computers and information technology, electrical consumer goods and service industries such as travel and tourism, hotels and restaurants.

If you are looking for information about particular careers including the qualifications, skills and experience required, there are several publications which can help which include *The A-Z of Careers and Jobs*, written by Diane Burston, published by Kogan Page and *Careers Encyclopaedia* written by Audrey Segal and Katherine Lea and published by Cassell.

## Temporary employment and interim management

For some people, temporary employment serves a useful purpose. If you are unemployed and looking for permanent work then you still need sufficient income to cover your expenses. Temporary work can also provide an important break from the boredom of unemployment. Details of your local employment agencies can be found in the *Yellow Pages*.

'Interim management' is a term applied to the recruitment of people on a temporary basis to fill key management positions. Many companies take the view that it is bad practice and commercially damaging to leave senior posts empty for six months or more while a permanent replacement is recruited.

*Manage Your Career*

In such cases, an interim manager can fill the gap.

Those who register as interim managers are not usually looking for permanent employment. In fact, they are more often retired and highly experienced managers who enjoy the freedom of working two or more days a week on assignments lasting from a week to several months. If you are interested in interim management, further information can be obtained from the Association of Temporary and Interim Executive Services (ATIES), 36-38 Mortimer Street, London W1N 7RN Tel: 0171 323 4300. Details of companies offering interim management services can also be found in *The Personnel Manager's Yearbook* published by AP Information Services, Roman House, 296 Golders Green Road, London NW11 9PZ Tel: 0181 455 4550.

## *Self-employment*

Nothing requires more thought than the step into self-employment because you are usually risking everything that you have. Many people have failed at it and many have succeeded. For those who do succeed it can provide a deeper and more varied satisfaction than anything else they may have undertaken.

You need certain strengths and qualities to succeed with self-employment and you need to choose the right field to enter just as carefully. All of this is discussed in more detail in Chapter 16: Working for Yourself.

## *Voluntary work*

Another challenge is to become involved in your community. The voluntary sector can be as gratifying as your professional work if you approach it with the same kind of commitment.

If you have no need to generate an income but want to give

your time, experience and skills to the benefit of those less fortunate than yourself, then working in the voluntary sector may be just the thing for you. See Chapter 17 for a list of useful addresses.

## Further Education
Continuous learning is what you need for continuous challenge. You can upgrade and extend job skills, or follow shifting career interests to improve the likelihood of doing new work. You can also learn for learning's sake.

There are many thousands of mature students enrolled in college courses all over the country. Some seek self-understanding, some want higher degrees in their current careers, while others are training for change or second careers. Still others are fulfilling a long-suppressed curiosity about the world and the people in it. Details of courses can often be found in local newspapers, libraries or from colleges themselves. Some courses can be directly geared to furthering a career. The Master of Business Administration is a good example. MBAs are available at more than 100 institutions nationwide, but only one third of these are accredited by the Association of MBAs.

For those with a thirst to learn but who prefer to study from home, the Association of British Correspondence Colleges offers hundreds of courses in everything from accountancy to zoo management. It also offers GCSEs, A-levels and vocational courses. As well as the traditional correspondence route, students can also join classes on interactive computer disks, and there are plans for lessons to be run on the Internet, to make distance learning accessible worldwide.

For those who want to develop degree-level skills, but cannot attend an institution full-time, the Open University is the best route. More than 143,000 people study with the Open University.

Before embarking on any of these routes it is a good idea to assess your own strengths and weaknesses and to apply a little lateral thinking to generate new and less obvious ideas for change. The next chapter: 'The Importance of Knowing Yourself' will help you with this process.

FRIEND: "HOW DO YOU LIKE YOUR CHANGE FROM SALESMAN TO POLICEMAN?"

NEW POLICEMAN: "FINE, THE PAY IS REGULAR AND THE HOURS ARE SATISFACTORY, BUT WHAT I LIKE BEST IS THAT THE CUSTOMER IS ALWAYS WRONG."

# 5

# The Importance of Knowing Yourself

*'Knowing myself intimately, I am able to take a more sympathetic view of myself than other people do'*
Robert Lynd

## Transferable Skills

Understanding yourself, including your strengths and weaknesses, is a very important part of the job-search process. For some people, the perception of themselves is narrow and self-limiting, and a consequence of feeling stuck and unskilled in some way at that moment in time. One way of breaking through this and understanding yourself better is to create a broader, fuller picture of what you can do, particularly concentrating on your transferable skills. As their name implies, these are the skills that are transferable from one job to another, from one field to another and from one career to another. Once you have mastered a skill in one job, you can easily transfer it to a different job and use it there.

The word 'skill' is a much misunderstood word in the world of work, often inaccurately presented in the following descriptions:

| | |
|---|---|
| A good mixer | Imaginative |
| Sympathetic | Intuitive |

Calm under pressure   Tolerant of others
Dynamic   Reliable
Decisive   Firm-minded
Determined

These are *not* skills, but rather the style with which you use your skills. Described as traits or temperaments, they can be measured by the Myers-Briggs Type Indicator, a popular test with recruiters. However, skills are in fact proficiencies or special abilities in a particular activity, whether naturally occurring or acquired by training.

Before you begin to consider your skills, take note of the following pointers:

- Set aside fears of being proud or boastful
- Do not assess or criticise your thoughts
- Consider the past and present – what you might be able to do already, or what you would like to learn
- Look for hidden potential

## *Types of Skill*

Types of skill can be broken down into a number of families or prime skills as follows:

> Intellectual skills
> Artistic skills
> Creative skills
> Communication and behavioural skills
> Managing/leading skills
> Manual skills
> Administrative/clerical skills

## The Importance of Knowing Yourself

Each family has skills ranging from simple to complex. Using a blank sheet of paper, write down the broadest possible range of skills, talents, abilities, strengths and resources you possess. You will find the inventory of skills below helpful in adding to your list.

| | |
|---|---|
| Achieving | Documenting |
| Actioning | Drafting reports |
| Advising others | Driving |
| Analysing | Editing documents |
| Arranging social events | Encouraging |
| Assembling | Erecting |
| Building | Establishing |
| Calculating numerical data | Fact-finding |
| Checking for accuracy | Fitting |
| Classifying records | Handling complaints |
| Coaching others | Influencing |
| Communicating | Initiating |
| Compiling figures | Inspecting |
| Constructing buildings | Instructing |
| Contacting | Interpreting data |
| Co-ordinating | Interviewing people |
| Corresponding with customers | Investigating |
| Counselling | Leading |
| Data gathering | Liaising |
| Decision making | Listening |
| Delegating responsibility | Machining |
| Designing | Maintaining records |
| Developing | Making |
| Directing | Managing |
| Dispensing information | Mediating between people |
| | Monitoring |

Motivating others
Negotiating
Observing
Obtaining
Operating equipment
Optimising
Organising people and work
Perfecting
Persuading others
Planning agendas
Preparing charts
Problem-solving
Programming computers
Promoting events
Protecting property
Raising funds
Recording data

Rectifying
Repairing
Researching
Reviewing
Running meetings
Selling
Serving the public
Shaping
Speaking in public
Summarising
Supervising staff
Teaching
Testing
Training
Troubleshooting
Visualising
Writing

## Ranking Your Skills

For anyone considering a career change, the process of ranking in order your transferable skills is most important. It will ultimately help to determine what job and career you choose. Your likes and dislikes must also feature strongly in your ranking otherwise you will not be happy with your final choice.

Also, whilst it is not always possible to get a job that uses *all* your transferable skills, you will want to take care that you are pursuing a job which at least allows you to use the most important of your skills. Ranking your skills has the added benefit of helping you to describe yourself during a job interview because you will be able to readily identify your greatest strengths and abilities.

Look at your list and consider how well each skill is developed. Which skills have not been put to use as often as you would like? Which skills would you like to develop more fully? Now prioritise them in order of importance to you and identify your top ten skills.

## Fleshing Out Your Skills

Having identified your top ten transferable skills using the one- or two-word descriptions suggested overleaf, you now need to flesh out your description of each skill. To do this you will need to compile a further list of your experience and accomplishments. Start by listing all your employers including dates and job titles. Against each job title think in terms of what you did and what you feel you accomplished. At this stage do not be selective – the important point is not to miss anything out.

Once you have compiled a list of your experience and accomplishments you can turn back to fleshing out your top ten transferable skills by adding the skill *object* and *how*. If, for example, one of your skills is problem-solving, then that's fine, but it doesn't really say very much. Using your experience and accomplishments should help you to describe the *object* or in this case, the type of problems you are capable of solving. In this way you could identify problem-solving associated with people, manufacturing, computers or finance, all of which require different skills.

The method you employ is the *how* of problem-solving. You may be good at solving people problems but what techniques do you use? You could say, 'I solve people problems effectively by listening to all the evidence before making a judgement', or 'I solve people problems effectively because I won't be rushed into making quick decisions'. Whilst these are describing the same skill, it is the *how* which makes you different from other people. Faced with a job interview it is often the *how* which sets you apart from any other applicant with the same skill.

Now apply the *object* and *how* to each of the top ten transferable skills on your list.

To round off your skills list we need to go back to the word *style* mentioned earlier in this chapter. In the context of skill, style simply helps a potential employer to understand what sets you apart from any other applicants with the same skill. Applied to the earlier example of problem-solving, you might wish to say 'I solve people problems effectively by listening to all the evidence before making a judgement, and remaining calm under pressure'. When appropriate, you can now apply *style* to each of your top ten transferable skills on your list.

Identifying your transferable skills is very important if you wish to succeed with your job search, so you must take your time to get it right. It may help if you ask someone else to tell you what they regard as your transferable skills. This should be someone you can trust to be honest and appreciative, such as your partner or close friend.

## Strengths v Weaknesses

Most of the things that you generally consider as weaknesses, if looked at in a different light, can actually be classed as strengths. For example, some people see themselves as indecisive. To others they appear careful; they avoid rash decisions. This strength is often valued in a job where the employer is looking for a meticulous employee. Why not spend some time considering your weaknesses and convert them into strengths.

As with your transferable skills, your relatives and friends can often help with this because they are more inclined to see you in the best light, whereas you may be over-critical about your own strengths and weaknesses.

## Searching for other Strengths

You may also have other strengths outside the field of employment that are demonstrated in your personal interests or hobbies. People often overlook time spent on fund-raising committees, as a school governor or as a regular visitor to the local hospice. All of these activities bring out additional strengths which are important to your job search.

# Part Two

# GETTING THE JOB YOU WANT

# 6

# Planning For Success

*'I like work, it fascinates me. I can sit and look at it for hours'*
*Three Men in a Boat*, Jerome K. Jerome

## Getting a job is a job in itself

Job hunting can be a lengthy process involving a considerable workload. Without good organisation you may find that you are often duplicating tasks or tackling too much at once so that nothing gets done thoroughly. Successful job hunters plan their campaigns in a professional manner, giving it as much priority as they would an important project in the workplace.

## From Your Personal Viewpoint

A disciplined approach will give you direction and control and it will help to maintain momentum and your morale, reducing the element of chance and enable you to exploit opportunities as they arise.

This disciplined approach has to apply to those around you as well. They have to understand the importance and the time element involved in your search for a job. Setting 'office' hours for your job search and days for interests and your partner and children, can help you and your family through this difficult time. Also, as you will be working from home quite a lot, don't forget to respect the life and space your partner and family need; they will not be used to having you around the house quite so much.

Never delude yourself into thinking there is plenty of time – there generally isn't! Too many people choose to take time out for a holiday, to paint the outside of their house or install a pond in their garden. The clock is always ticking and before you can turn around one month will have become six and you will be in a weaker financial position. If you really need a holiday, the time to take it is between accepting and starting a new job.

Set personal daily and weekly targets which include priorities, and don't put anything off until tomorrow that you can do today. When you prioritise activities, the key question to keep asking yourself is 'is this the best way to use my time?' One method you could try using is to identify those tasks which could be scheduled (proactive tasks) and those which crop up as unscheduled (reactive tasks). Allot time to each of the proactive tasks based on their importance and plan a few free slots to fit in reactive tasks. If any reactive task turns out to be urgent or important then you may have to reschedule.

Consider your search for a job as like being in business on your own, where you are in competition with others to win your next order, or in this case your next job. Always keep a good standard of dress and appearance, this is important for your own self-esteem as much as for the affect it has on those around you.

## Space of Your Own

For effective job search you need your own space in the house, ideally as quiet and private as possible. A spare bedroom would be ideal for this purpose, but clearly this may be difficult if you are married with two children and live in a small property. If a spare room isn't available, then come to an arrangement with your spouse that you will use a particular room as your office for certain hours every day. This really is very important, because without space of your own you will find it difficult to maintain any kind of routine; you will lose interest in the job search process, experience frustration and family hostility.

You are going to need a desk or table, a telephone, and a good supply of stationery and postage stamps. Invest in quality paper and envelopes – creating a good impression is very important for successful job searching.

Provide yourself with a good size desk diary. It is vital that your family knows where you are and when you are likely to return in case there is a telephone call from an employer or recruitment consultant. Explain to your family the importance of answering the telephone correctly and taking messages. Make sure that the area around your telephone is kept clear of obstructions, that there is a copy of your CV close to hand and a notepad and pen.

If you have your own computer with word-processing software or an electronic typewriter you are well on the way to producing quality CVs and correspondence. If you don't have this equipment, find someone who has and persuade them to help you with your job search. It would be worth paying them an hourly fee for this support.

You are going to have to set up an effective filing system. This is vital if you are going to cope with a large number of applications. Many of the positions you apply for will be similar, so you need to keep track and maintain access to your previous applications and approaches. On the following page is a suggested format.

## JOB APPLICATION PROGRESS SHEET

| Date of Application | Company Name | Advert or Speculative | Position Location | Reply Received | Follow-up Date | First Interview | Second Interview | Result |
|---|---|---|---|---|---|---|---|---|
| | | | | | | | | |
| | | | | | | | | |
| | | | | | | | | |
| | | | | | | | | |
| | | | | | | | | |
| | | | | | | | | |
| | | | | | | | | |
| | | | | | | | | |
| | | | | | | | | |
| | | | | | | | | |
| | | | | | | | | |
| | | | | | | | | |
| | | | | | | | | |

## Establishing an Office Routine

Prioritising your job search activities should include establishing a daily office routine. The routine below is an example which you may like to adapt to your own circumstances.

---

**Example of an Office Routine**
**AM**

✓ Deal with today's mail.
✓ Prepare CVs and letters of application in response to previous day's advertisements.
✓ Prepare speculative letters to employers.
✓ Prepare speculative letters to recruitment consultants.
✓ Make follow-up telephone calls to earlier contacts.
✓ Complete any administrative matters such as personal tax, car and life insurance.

**Lunchbreak**

**PM**

✓ Visit library to read advertisements in local and national newspapers, trade and professional journals, conduct research etc.
✓ Write up observations from recent interviews.
✓ Prepare for future interviews including travel arrangements.
✓ Write follow-up letters for interviews attended or make telephone calls.
✓ Check the diary.
✓ Post the mail.

Don't be put off by the demand all of this places on your time. Self-discipline and commitment will reap the benefits of a well-organised job search and will help you to retain the motivation you need to keep going.

# 7

# Researching the Job Market

> *'One can only rest after plenty of practice'*
> George Ade

Once you've identified the job you really want, you are ready to begin researching the job market. Expanding your knowledge in this way will open up many more opportunities in your job search.

## Identifying potential employers

Finding out about potential employers, their products, services and general background is invaluable in terms of generating speculative applications, responding to job advertisements and in preparation for interviews. Most of the following literature you will need can be found in the reference section of your main or central library and you will find the librarian very helpful if you explain what you are looking for.

Your aim is to identify and build information on the type of companies in your chosen geographic area. Use a separate sheet of paper for each company and copy all the relevant information you can find. This should include name, address and telephone number of the company; the name of any holding company or group; the names and titles of directors or senior managers including the senior personnel management or human resources job; a description of the company's services or products; the size of the company in turnover and staff numbers and the location of all its premises. Finally include any other information you can find about recent company developments, achievements or acquisitions.

Only by carrying out this research can you hope to identify the employers who are a good fit for you and your job search. The more information you can obtain, the better, since you can now personalise any letter of application, whether speculative or in response to a job advertisement. In addition, your research will contribute greatly towards creating a good impression when you are selected for interview.

*KOMPASS Register of British Industry & Commerce*
Gives details of Britain's leading 42,000 companies. As well as address, telephone number and products/services, Kompass gives names of directors and executives, turnover and the number of employees. The directory is the official register of the CBI (Confederation of British Industry); all member firms are included and are specifically marked. There are three sections to *KOMPASS*:

Section One    –    Products & Services
Section Two    –    Company information
Section Three  –    Financial data

As you will probably wish to find companies which manufacture specific products or provide specific services you are best to start at the beginning of Section One. Each product or service is given a number. Once you have the numbers you want the relevant companies producing these products or services can be found in the remainder of Section One and all of Section Two. Section Three will provide useful financial information.

*Key British Companies*
Provides up-to-date profiles of the top 50,000 companies in the UK. Each entry gives financial data, details of trading names and functions and other data designed to enable the user to make concise assessment of a company's size and range of activities. It also includes the names of key personnel.

*The Times 1000*
The core of this directory is the list of the 1,000 largest UK companies, ranked by total turnover. Other information includes details of main activity, chairman, capital employed, net profit and number of employees.

*Who Owns Whom*
Designed to help anyone needing information about company connections. Volume One indexes parent companies followed by subsidiaries. Volume Two lists subsidiaries followed by their parent company. Updated quarterly, *Who Owns Whom* is a valuable source of information on recent takeovers and mergers.

*Stock Exchange Official Yearbook*
A source of information on some 3,000 listed companies. It gives the names of directors plus considerable financial data.

*Britain's Privately Owned Companies*
Useful source of information about privately owned companies ranked by sales.

*Kelly's Manufacturers and Merchants Directory*
Includes manufacturers, merchants, wholesalers and companies offering any industrial service. Over 80,000 companies are listed giving name, address, telephone number and a brief description.

*The City Directory*
Very comprehensive listing of finance-orientated organisations.

*Directory of British Associations*
An important source when seeking specialist advice and information. It gives details of interests, membership, activities and publications of 6,300 specialist associations.

*Major Companies of Europe*
(Formerly *Principal Companies of the EEC*). Lists over 4,000 of western Europe's largest companies, detailing boards, senior executives, principal activities, subsidiaries, trade names and certain financial information.

*McCarthy UK Quoted and Unquoted Service*
Prior to an interview, you can obtain useful copy text of newspaper articles which have appeared about the company in question (only available in larger libraries).

*The Personnel Manager's Yearbook*
This brings together key contact information on the UK's 8,000 largest companies and organisations. The minimum information is the name of the chief executive, the person responsible for the personnel function, the number of employees and the company activity. Subsidiaries as well as parent companies can also be found. In addition to the employer

information, there is a list of recruitment consultants and agencies, management consultants and training organisations.

*Confederations of Chambers of Commerce Directory*
This is a useful source, but you may only be able to find a directory covering the specific part of the country in which you live, for example the North West or Central Southern England. Each directory lists chamber member companies of all sizes with name, address, telephone number and activity. Some libraries can provide a smaller directory for a specific city or town and these will include name, address, telephone number, activity and a contact name.

*Local Council Directories*
Often produced by the planning departments of local councils these publications list companies with contact names.

Finally, don't forget the *Yellow Pages* and *Thomson Directories*.

# PC Information on Employers

A much more recent development is that of obtaining *The Times* and *Daily Telegraph* by quarterly subscription on CD-ROM software. This is expensive, even if you have your own PC, but you may just find that your library has made the investment. This is very useful if you are researching a smaller group of employers to approach on a speculative basis or are preparing for an interview. With CD-ROM it is possible to input the name of the company together with certain key words, such as 'finance' or 'expansion' and the software will produce the company articles containing these key words which can then be printed off.

# 8

# Compiling your Curriculum Vitae

*'Every brand of knowledge which a man possesses, he may apply to some good purpose'*

C. Buchanan

## Which CVs Win Interviews?

One thing most employers would agree on is that too many people take the term curriculum vitae too literally. This Latin phrase means the course of (one's) life and that is precisely what some people's CVs become – sometimes stretching to ten or more pages. However in recruitment circles the term refers not so much to the course of (one's) life but to a history of your career – its purpose is to introduce you to a potential employer and win an interview.

In today's climate finding a job is both challenging and taxing. So, it is important that you don't waste your time sending out poorly prepared CVs by the sackful. Instead, think of your CV as a personal selling document, and a properly prepared one will form an essential part of your job-search plan.

There are no fixed rules on the completion of CVs. However, you will no doubt be given well meaning advice from friends and relatives. Consider carefully before acting on any of this advice. Remember, the one and only true test of a good CV is whether it gets you an interview.

First impressions count! A CV is often the first information the prospective employer will see. Think of the person who will receive your CV – put yourself in their shoes and you will begin to understand the importance of this document. Employers receive hundreds of CVs in response to job advertisements, not counting the hundreds they receive as speculative enquiries. That's a lot of reading. So your CV has to stand out if it is to get beyond first base. Whilst the CV is only part of the selection process, it is the one part over which you can have complete control. No one gets a job because of their CV, but it can get you an interview, which is your first achievement in applying for any job.

In many companies the first sifting process is undertaken by someone from the Personnel or Human Resources department. These people do not have the authority to decide who will be appointed, but quite often they do decide who will be interviewed. Knowing this is important, because yet again, it is a clue to the techniques to be used when constructing your CV.

So how do these Personnel and HR people go about the business of selecting who should be interviewed? Well, because of the volume of CVs received by any one employer, their objective is to reduce the number of applications from several hundred to a manageable eight or so for interview. Recruiters therefore look for reasons to *reject* applications not reasons to put applications on the 'for interview' pile. What can the jobhunter do to make their CV stand out from all the others and what can be done to minimise the risk of rejection?

Your CV is your career history, so you should keep it brief – normally no more than two sides of A4. Don't be tempted to give a blow-by-blow account of your life story, or a long list of responsibilities from your previous job description. You will bore the recruiter very quickly, many of whom are put off by lengthy autobiographies. As a result it is much more likely that he or she will find a reason to put your CV in the 'for rejection' pile.

It would appear that when faced with several hundred CVs, the recruiter will give each one no more than a 30-second scan. To minimise the risk of rejection you should therefore only include enough information to whet the appetite and enable the recruiter to think 'I must see this candidate'.

So what should be left out? Good sense suggests that you should leave out anything that is negative or superfluous. Negative information will be particularly damaging to your application at the CV stage. Let's assume your CV achieves an interview. If you left one of your employers because of a disagreement with your boss and you are asked about your reasons for leaving that particular job at the interview, then at least you will have a far better chance of fully explaining this event in terms which are not damaging to your application. So think very very carefully about the content of your CV – and when in doubt, leave it out!

Remember that recruiters are not always realistic about age and educational requirements when they advertise, so don't be put off if you feel confident about the recruiter's other criteria. If you are concerned that factors such as age and lack of formal qualifications may not go in your favour, then relegate this information to its rightful place – on the back page. If the recruiter is impressed with your achievements, experience and skills on the first page, they will mentally peg you as a candidate for interview and are less likely to be bothered by what they read later on.

Of course your CV should be neat, easy to read and well laid out, and we will deal with these aspects later in the chapter. However there is much more to a good CV if it is to succeed in getting beyond this rather negative vetting process.

## The personal profile

One quite recent trend which will help to get your CV noticed is to include a personal profile.

A personal profile is a word picture or brief statement of your job skills, experience, abilities and personal skills. The ideal structure should be no more than three short paragraphs of information in which you can sell yourself to the employer. What you are in fact saying is 'this is what I have to offer you, these are the benefits you would gain from employing me'.

The only place for a personal profile is the beginning of your CV. Here it will have maximum impact and the recruiter will feel drawn towards the text. The aim is to hook the reader and retain their interest. They will feel compelled to read on and may be less bothered by information later in your CV that is not such a close match to their requirements.

Earlier in this book you have been encouraged to spend time cataloguing your experience, skills and abilities, achievements, strengths and personal characteristics. Use this information to prepare your personal profile. The time and effort spent constructing your personal profile can give you confidence in yourself, and encourages better self-knowledge. You will end up better prepared to use this information in letters of application, telephone conversations with employers and recruitment consultancies, and in response to searching questions at the interview stage.

The question of whether you use the personal profile technique must be yours to answer. It is a powerful tool in getting your CV noticed, but as it becomes more and more prevalent, recruiters may become too familiar with this technique and hence less impressed. So you must decide whether it is truly an appropriate technique for you and the job for which you are applying. If you opt to include a personal profile then striking the right balance with the content is essential, or its use may be counterproductive.

To help you get the general idea of how to construct a personal profile, some examples have been included on the following pages.

## Examples of personal profiles

*A capable and enthusiastic law graduate who has recently completed the Law Society Finals Course, now seeking a first appointment in a law firm, where training and development are important to career progression.*

*Resourceful and a positive thinker who is well able to absorb facts and details together with the ability to draw conclusions and make recommendations. Reliable and adaptable with a resilient approach to work.*

*An articulate person with good listening and observing skills who can advise and mediate between others. Sociable and able to mix well.*

\*

*This person has had a successful career within finance and administration, and has developed and shown a steady and regular pattern of achievement and increasing responsibility. Capable of absorbing facts and details and of working to strict deadlines.*

*Numerate and literate with sound written abilities in the presentation of reports and a strong eye for detail. A self-motivated person with good organising skills and an open-minded approach to problem-solving.*

\*

*An Operations Manager with 18 years experience in three major companies. Played a significant role in establishing a total quality management programme, improving employee morale and communications and introduced new production methods.*

*A very capable and effective team-builder, managing and motivating others. Has a positive attitude to problem-solving and remains calm in times of stress. Organising is a particular strong point as is the ability to work to tight deadlines.*

\*

*An experienced personnel generalist with a particularly strong background in developing personnel policies and procedures. Used to working at a strategic level as well as using a more 'hands-on' approach at an operational level.*

*Has excellent interpersonal and presentation skills and adaptable enough to be able to work on his own and as part of a team. Can demonstrate an effective record of implementing new Human Resources initiatives.*

\*

*A very capable, successful and self-motivated sales professional, who works well on his own or as an efficient member of a team.*

*A high achiever with excellent negotiation and customer contact skills and a successful track record of developing new sales opportunities. A resourceful and positive-thinker who is diplomatic and tactful when dealing with people, but whose determination and enthusiasm produces excellent results. A sound communicator with an ability to relate at all levels and capable of working to tight deadlines.*

## How to Make a Start with Achievements

Begin by cataloguing in a logical and orderly fashion all your personal information, education, qualifications and training. Then put together your career information, your job titles, who you worked for and when, and record all your experience, specialist knowledge, skills, abilities, strengths and achievements and important personal qualities.

You will almost certainly have assembled far more information than you can possibly include. Don't worry! This additional information will prove very useful, particularly at the interview stage.

Responsibilities are fine, but they never have the same impact as achievements. Listing responsibilities merely reflects what your employer asked you to do not what you may have actually done, or for that matter, how well you performed these tasks. Recruiters find such CVs dull and uninteresting, so it figures that jobhunters who list their previous successes and achievements can be sure of their CV standing out from the rest.

Think carefully about the word *achievement*; the dictionary defines the word as 'something that has been accomplished successfully, especially by means of skill, effort, practice or perseverance'. Start the process by taking a careful look at your career for evidence of previous successes. Focus more on what is recent rather than what is distant and therefore perhaps less important. Pick out the highlights of your jobs and those things you did particularly well or that you feel proud of. Did you introduce anything new for an employer, perhaps a piece of equipment, a process or procedure? Did you perform so well that your employer actually benefited from it? Did you continually exceed a performance target or reduce costs? These questions will help to prompt you to formulate ideas of your own and to recognise the sort of things which recruiters are influenced by when they examine CVs.

So, besides being neat, easy to read and well laid out, the winning quality needed is that you shine out above the rest. Remember, don't hide your light under a bushel; your achievements, if presented properly, will improve your CV immensely.

Once you're satisfied with your list of achievements, you will need to analyse each one to draw out further benefits to the potential employer. Concentrate on the end results, not the means. Attaching a number to each achievement gives it more impact and makes it much more believable, convincing and readily understood. So, whenever possible, quantify your achievements using numbers, volume or monetary value.

At this stage you should also ask yourself 'how did my employer benefit from this achievement?' This is often quite difficult to answer, but you will find the effort well worthwhile. It adds an extra dimension to your achievements and is useful preparation for future interviews.

Here are some examples of achievements including both these principles:

- Improved quality systems and procedures resulting in a reduction in the customer complaint level of 60 per cent, achieving more repeat orders and better customer retention figures.
- Introduced new procedures and management training to deal with absenteeism cutting the annual number of days lost by 50 per cent.

- Carried out a major review of transport operations and all associated costs, reducing workforce and vehicles with a subsequent saving to the company of £385k.
- Consistently exceeded sales budget by 20 per cent, increasing the number of new customers and improving the company's market share.
- Improved telephone answering response to 15 seconds or less for all calls, increasing staff morale and customer retention levels.

An important aspect of style, particularly when you're writing about your achievements, is the use of the *immediate past tense*. This enables you to avoid using the *first person singular*. With space at a premium it makes sense to omit all the 'I' references and it gives your achievements a sense of completion, which is just the impression you wish to convey.

Stick to plain and simple language the reader will understand, and don't use business jargon or words only you and your previous employer would be familiar with. Ex-service personnel should take particular care.

Don't be tempted to be pompous or humorous. The chances are this will fail to impress the recruiter who won't want to take chances.

To help you construct your list of achievements here is a list of action verbs, but make sure when using these words that they are used properly and create the right impression.

| | | |
|---|---|---|
| Accelerated | Advanced | Arranged |
| Accomplished | Advised | Assembled |
| Achieved | Analysed | Assessed |
| Adapted | Approved | Attained |
| Administered | Arbitrated | Balanced |

| | | |
|---|---|---|
| Benefited | Executed | Motivated |
| Challenged | Expanded | Negotiated |
| Channelled | Extended | Observed |
| Coached | Financed | Obtained |
| Collaborated | Formulated | Operated |
| Commissioned | Founded | Ordered |
| Communicated | Gained | Organised |
| Compiled | Gathered | Originated |
| Completed | Generated | Participated |
| Conceived | Identified | Perfected |
| Consolidated | Implemented | Performed |
| Controlled | Improved | Persuaded |
| Created | Incorporated | Pioneered |
| Defined | Increased | Planned |
| Delivered | Influenced | Predicted |
| Demonstrated | Inspected | Prepared |
| Directed | Inspired | Presented |
| Displayed | Installed | Processed |
| Diverted | Instigated | Produced |
| Doubled | Integrated | Programmed |
| Edited | Introduced | Projected |
| Eliminated | Invented | Promoted |
| Enabled | Investigated | Provided |
| Enforced | Judged | Publicised |
| Engineered | Liaised | Purchased |
| Enhanced | Launched | Questioned |
| Enriched | Maintained | Realised |
| Established | Managed | Reasoned |
| Estimated | Manipulated | Recommended |
| Evaluated | Marketed | Reconciled |
| Examined | Minimised | Recorded |
| Exceeded | Monitored | Recruited |

*Compiling your Curriculum Vitae*

| | | |
|---|---|---|
| Reduced | Simplified | Tested |
| Referred | Sold | Traded |
| Reported | Solved | Trained |
| Researched | Specialised | Transferred |
| Resolved | Sponsored | Transformed |
| Restored | Started | Translated |
| Restructured | Streamlined | Tutored |
| Retrieved | Strengthened | Understudied |
| Reviewed | Structured | Undertook |
| Scheduled | Succeeded | Upgraded |
| Secured | Summarised | Used |
| Selected | Supervised | Utilised |
| Serviced | Supplied | Worked |
| Shaped | Terminated | |

Now that you have your list of achievements, it is important to include only those that are truly relevant to the job for which you are applying. In fact, the more you can personalise your achievements to seem exactly what the employer is looking for in the job advertisement or job description, for example, the better.

Rank order your list of achievements in the order you believe the recruiter would wish to see them – use the job advertisement or job description to help you with this.

Finally, whilst an achievement-based CV has many advantages, don't forget the recruiter's 30-second scan and make sure that every word counts!

## Other Useful tips

Staying with the strategy of only including that information which will maximise your chances of selection, here are a few tips on things to leave out:

- **Your age**
  I mentioned the need for caution on this subject earlier in this section. Only ever put your date of birth and consider putting this on the back page.
- **Ages of children**
  I must also caution you against including the age(s) of your child(ren), particularly if they are of school age or younger. Recruiters can have their prejudices too, and some believe that applicants with children do not have the same level of commitment.
- **Names of referees**
  At this stage referees are completely unnecessary.
- **Photographs**
  Possibly one of the best ways of influencing the recruiter in the wrong direction! Few of us are really photogenic and we also put ourselves at the mercy of the recruiter's inbuilt prejudices of what constitutes a 'safe face'.
- **Salary**
  Never, never include salary. Do so at the CV stage and you are leaving yourself open to early rejection. Most employers want the best candidate they can get for only enough money to attract, motivate and retain you. So why give away one of your best means of negotiation?

## Leisure Interests

Leisure interest can often make a difference in the eye of the recruiter, but only if they can be seen to support your application. If you have other achievements, apart from work, for example school governor, secretary of local gardening club, fundraiser for local charity, manager of a local football team etc., they will send a certain signal to the recruiter. If you enjoy classical music, Roman history and collecting World War Two memorabilia then quite possibly you will send signals of a different type. You are helping the recruiter understand you, the applicant, your values and what motivates you. In this way, it can certainly be helpful to include how you spend your free time.

## CV Presentation

Quality of presentation affects greatly the impact your CV will have on the recruiter. You may be confident that the content is now spot on, but if you haven't taken the trouble to make sure it is presented properly you're wasting your time. Let's begin by examining structure or the order in which the sections of your CV appear.

The order of the sections is really up to you to decide, but because most people are employed for their experience and achievements I would suggest the following order:

- Start with your name, address and telephone number. It is no longer fashionable to start with the title Curriculum Vitae. Frankly, it is unnecessary and takes up valuable space.
- Personal Profile – Remember to consider carefully if this technique is right for you.
- Career and Achievements – in reverse chronological order list the names of your employers, with dates against each one, and under each employer put your appropriate achievements.
- Professional Qualifications and Training
- Education – start with your highest qualification first.
- Interests
- Personal information

Here are some further tips to help you with the presentation of your CV:

- Always have your CV typed or printed. If you have access to a personal computer with a word-processing package, and a printer with good letter quality output, so much the better. Choose a standard typeface and stick with it throughout the document. Don't mix typefaces. If you are unable to produce your own CV, consider employing someone to do this for you.
- Unless you can produce good photocopies, don't bother. The employer won't be impressed with poor quality photocopies.
- Always use good quality white paper – aim at 100 gramme.
- Don't use plastic folders and coloured covers – they aren't necessary and only add to the cost.
- Check your CV very carefully for spelling and grammatical mistakes – have someone else proofread your CV for these kind of errors.
- Send your CV in a strong A4 envelope – don't fold it. Always use a first-class stamp.

## Technology in selection

Recently, some employers and search-and-selection consultants have embarked on a totally new approach to the reading of CVs. Instead of the human reader they are using computers to read CVs via sophisticated high-speed scanners using optical character recognition (OCR) software. The level of specialization varies from a machine that searches for key words which the recruiter has specified, to a machine where the OCR software converts the scanned material into basic text format.

The system's artificial intelligence reads the text and extracts data, such as name, address, telephone number, skills, qualifications, previous employers and job titles, all with relevant dates.

The computer then reorganises this information into a standard format dictated by the recruiter and compares this with all the vacancies on the database.

This highly sophisticated computer system can recognise skills and qualifications regardless of how well they are written because it is not only comparing them with the thousands of words with which it is programmed but also their abbreviations, synonyms and acronyms.

A typical search might list a number of mandatory requirements such as qualifications, skills and a number of years experience followed by a list of preferred requirements. The system would then carry out a search, producing a list of applicants and ranking them by the number of preferred requirements that each fulfils.

It is important to recognise that the number of employers using this system is still quite small at present. However their numbers are on the increase and search and selection consultants are also taking a much greater interest in this recruitment tool – recruitment systems such as these are far better equipped than humans to evaluate large volumes of CVs.

What does all this mean for those who are preparing their CV? The greatest impact lies in the way the CV is constructed – placing a much greater emphasis on content and on key words within the areas of skills, knowledge and experience and also on style or layout. Whether you are responding to a specific advertisement or simply sending your CV on a speculative basis to an employer or consultant there is always the possibility that they may be using OCR software, unless the business is small.

Using a personal profile or summary at the beginning of the CV that includes the recruiter's key words is important. This can then be followed by the main body of the CV, where it is important to avoid repetition of these key words, using synonyms instead. Should the system not recognise the key words in the personal profile then there is a good chance it will recognise its synonyms in the body of the CV. Great care must be taken in preparing the content of your CV and making every word count.

The software used by these systems is confused by certain layouts and typefaces. In such cases, because the system cannot read the CV, it is unable to extract information and fails to produce anything to compare with the vacancies in the database.

To help overcome these problems, I have produced the following guidelines:

- Use a Sans Serif typeface such as Helvetica. Serifs are the little strokes at an angle to the vertical lines of a character that whilst pleasing to the human eye, confuse the OCR system.
- Don't underline or italicise; use capital letters or bold type for emphasis. To OCR software, underlinings and italics effectively join all the characters of the word into one.
- Don't place boxes around text, for example around the personal profile. Such boxes prevent the software from reading the text.
- CVs produced by dot-matrix printers tend to hinder the reading process, as do photocopies.
- Don't put text on both sides of a page because only one side can be scanned.

- Your name should be the first item on the CV. Address and telephone number should be next but not on the same line as your name.
- Always place dates *before* education and career history as this increases the chance of the computer reading the dates correctly.

## The Final Word

There is no single best way of drawing up a CV. Ultimately it is what you feel is best for you, and what you feel most comfortable with. Quite often it is a good idea to have more than one version of your CV. This enables you to highlight particular aspects of your career and to personalise it towards a particular job or employer. However, this is no easy task, and because you must always send your CV with a covering letter, whether you are applying for an advertised vacancy or sending a speculative application, then the next best thing is to personalise your letter. There are several ways of doing this, including a technique called the executive briefing. More about this can be found in Chapters 12 and 13.

*Manage Your Career*

# 9

# Vacancies – How and Where to Find Them

*'That's the reason they're called lessons,' the Gryphon remarked. 'Because they lessen from day to day.'*
*Alice in Wonderland* – Lewis Carroll

There are more sources of job vacancies than most people imagine. This chapter is devoted to opening your eyes not simply to the source of advertised vacancies but to the much larger source of unadvertised vacancies.

## Advertised Vacancies

Job vacancies can be found in the national dailies, weekend papers, in your regional and local papers and in trade or professional magazines. You need to find out which carry the job advertisements in which you are specifically interested. However at this stage don't be too selective, you could very easily miss that all too important job advert.

### National Newspapers
National newspapers, divided into three groups, popular, mid market and quality, are an important source of job advertisements. Some specialise in advertising jobs in particular sectors, whilst others carry all jobs across all sectors. It's also important to remember that some national newspapers have a

regional edition. This appeals to companies who specifically wish to attract candidates from the north or the south. The three national newspapers with a regional edition are:

| | | |
|---|---|---|
| Daily Mail | – | North, South. |
| The Express | – | North/Scottish, South. |
| The Sun | – | North, South, Scottish. |

On the following pages, arranged alphabetically, is a schedule of job sectors followed by the national newspapers that carry job advertisements for those sectors and the days of the week on which the advertisements appear. If you would prefer to carry out your job search in a different way, using national newspapers as the lead item rather than job sector, a schedule compiled in this way has been included in Chapter 17.

## Job Advertisements – Where and When to Find Them in the National Newspapers

| Job Sector | National Newspapers | Day of the Week |
|---|---|---|
| Accountancy | Financial Times Independent | Thursday Wednesday |
| Banking | Financial Times Independent | Wednesday Wednesday |
| Building and Construction | The Sun | Tuesday Thursday |

## Vacancies – How and Where to Find Them

| Job Sector | National Newspapers | Day of the Week |
|---|---|---|
| Careers | Guardian | Saturday |
| Catering/Hotels | The Express | Thursday |
| Creative & Media | Guardian | Monday |
| | Guardian | Saturday |
| | The Times | Friday |
| Education | Guardian | Tuesday |
| | Guardian | Saturday |
| | Independent | Thursday |
| | Scotsman | Wednesday |
| | The Times | Friday |
| Engineering | Daily Mail | Thursday |
| | The Express | Thursday |
| | The Sun | Thursday |
| Environment | Guardian | Wednesday |
| European | The European | Wednesday |
| Finance | Financial Times | Wednesday |
| | Financial Times | Thursday |
| | Independent | Wednesday |
| Financial Sales | The Express | Thursday |
| Fund raising | Guardian | Monday |
| General Appointments | Daily Mail | Thursday |
| | Daily Telegraph | Thursday |
| | Financial Times | Wednesday |
| | Guardian | Tuesday |
| | Guardian | Saturday |
| | Independent | Thursday |

*Manage Your Career*

| Job Sector | National Newspapers | Day of the Week |
|---|---|---|
| General Appointments | Independent on Sunday | Sunday |
| | Mail on Sunday | Sunday |
| | Scotsman | Monday through to Friday |
| | Sunday Times | Sunday |
| | The Express | Thursday |
| Graduate | Guardian | Saturday |
| | Independent | Thursday |
| Health | Guardian | Wednesday |
| Housing | Guardian | Wednesday |
| International | Sunday Telegraph | Sunday |
| | Sunday Times | Sunday |
| IT | Independent | Tuesday |
| | Observer | Sunday |
| | The Times | Wednesday |
| Legal | Independent | Wednesday |
| | The Times | Tuesday |
| Management/ Executive | Daily Telegraph | Thursday |
| | Independent on Sunday | Sunday |
| | Sunday Telegraph | Sunday |
| | Sunday Times | Sunday |
| | The Times | Thursday |
| Marketing | Guardian | Monday |

## Vacancies – How and Where to Find Them

| Job Sector | National Newspapers | Day of the Week |
|---|---|---|
| Marketing | The Scotsman | Friday |
|  | The Times | Friday |
| Multilingual | Independent | Wednesday |
|  | The European | Wednesday |
|  | The Times | Wednesday |
| Printing and Publishing | Daily Mail | Thursday |
| Public Relations | Guardian | Monday |
|  | Guardian | Saturday |
| Public Sector | Guardian | Wednesday |
|  | Guardian | Saturday |
|  | Scotsman | Thursday |
| Retail | Daily Mail | Thursday |
| Sales | Daily Mail | Thursday |
|  | Guardian | Monday |
|  | Guardian | Saturday |
|  | Scotsman | Friday |
|  | The Sun | Tuesday |
|  | The Sun | Thursday |
| Science | The Times | Friday |
| Secretarial | Guardian | Saturday |
|  | Daily Mail | Tuesday |
|  | Guardian | Monday |
|  | Independent | Wednesday |
|  | The Times | Wednesday |
|  | The Times | Thursday |

| Job Sector | National Newspapers | Day of the Week |
|---|---|---|
| Technical | Daily Mail | Thursday |
| | The Express | Thursday |
| | The Sun | Thursday |
| Training | The Times | Friday |
| All Sectors Covered | Daily Telegraph | Thursday |
| | Independent on Sunday | Sunday |
| | Mail on Sunday | Sunday |
| | Sunday Telegraph | Sunday |
| | Sunday Times | Sunday |
| | The Sun | Tuesday |
| | The Sun | Thursday |

## Regional Newspapers

Many companies prefer to advertise in their regional or local newspapers. They are published on a daily, evening or weekly basis, either paid for or free, and should be included as an important source of job vacancies.

The following selection of regional newspapers regularly carry quite a large number of job pages with good appointments sections:

Belfast Telegraph
Birmingham Evening Mail
Courier and Advertiser (Dundee)
Evening Chronicle (Newcastle)
Evening Standards (London)
Hull Daily Mail

*Vacancies – How and Where to Find Them*

Liverpool Echo
Manchester Evening News
Press and Journal (Aberdeen)
Shropshire Star
The Glasgow Herald
Yorkshire Evening Post

Remember, it can work out quite expensive if you opt to regularly buy national and regional newspapers. To keep your costs down, read the free copies available at your library as often as possible.

## *Trade and Professional Magazines*

Trade and professional magazines are also a very useful source of job advertisements. If you are professionally qualified, the chances are you will regularly receive your institute's magazine by post. If you don't qualify for a free copy, I suggest you ask your library for a publication called BRAD (British Rate and Data). This is a classified directory of media in the UK that carry advertising. There is a section dedicated to business titles where you can search for the magazines appropriate to your professional or industry. Check if your library has a copy of your chosen magazine. If not, do you have any contacts who may be able to pass their copy on to you? Alternatively, it may be worth your while purchasing several months' copies to help with your job search.

Here are some examples of professional magazine titles:

Computer Weekly
Professional Builder
Management Accounting
Farmers Weekly

Nursing Times
People Management
Accountancy Age
The Grocer
Professional Engineer
New Civil Engineer
The Pharmaceutical
The Gas Installer

## The Internet

Advertising jobs on the Internet is proving to be popular with most recruitment agencies and recruitment consultants who are able to post advertisements on their web pages within 15 minutes of being told of the vacancy. In a recent survey, 30 per cent of recruitment agencies placed jobs on the Internet, with nine out of ten expecting to see a growing number of vacancies advertised in this way. Relatively few employers currently advertise on the Internet, but many more may come round to using this particular recruitment technique.

If you have a powerful enough home computer with a modem, you could subscribe to one of the online service providers such as CompuServe, AOL and BT Internet. This would enable you to access recruitment agencies with websites such as Interworknet and Jobnet. Whilst there is no charge for this service, you must take into account the subscription to the online service provider and the cost of additional telephone calls.

Once you are through to your chosen website, you will find hundreds of vacancies grouped into job types. The first thing you will notice is that the description for each job is quite small compared with an advertisement in the newspaper.

Make a note of the vacancies in which you are interested together with any reference number and telephone the recruitment agency for more information. You should find the agency helpful, since it is in their interest to find candidates who are a good match for their client's requirements.

# Recruitment Specialists

## Headhunters

Search consultants, often called headhunters, are generally used by an employer when the number of potential job holders is limited either because of the speciality of the job or the seniority of the post. The headhunter's role, when presented with an assignment by a client, is to identify and track down likely candidates who may be currently employed, and perhaps not actively seeking a change of job, so not reading the appointments section in the national newspapers.

From the employer's viewpoint, using a headhunter has the advantage of being totally confidential, but the downside is that the candidate has to be tempted into making a move sometimes at a salary level outside the employer's initial limits. Despite this drawback, it is estimated that among 65-75 per cent of vacancies are not advertised.

If you receive a telephone call from a headhunter, he or she will ask whether you are in a position to talk. If you have someone with you or the timing is inconvenient, then ask him for his telephone number and tell him you'll call back or alternatively ask him to call you on your home number outside of office hours.

Once you are free to talk, the headhunter will probably arrange an interview. This will differ from a typical employer interview because most headhunters work on the basis that by the time they call someone to come in, they already know a great deal about them from their research.

Most interviews with headhunters can be quite lengthy, anything between one and two hours, with some taking even longer. A more recent trend is to include the taking of a battery of psychometric tests and attendance at an assessment centre.

If you are unemployed, you may wonder how an approach from a headhunter is relevant to you since they tend to set their sights on candidates in employment. The fact is that times are changing. There are a lot of very good unemployed people in the job market and consequently many of today's headhunters are open minded enough to include them in their searches.

Can you make direct approaches to headhunters? Well, of course you can. If you can get hold of a copy of the *CEPEC Recruitment Guide* this lists recruitment agencies and search consultants. Select those who operate in your industry or business area and send them a copy of your CV. Don't be put off when you hear stories that some headhunters receive hundreds of unsolicited CVs. It is an essential part of your job search plan to get your CV registered with headhunters but do take care to follow the advice in Chapter 8 on CV preparation, paying particular attention to making yours achievement-orientated.

## Recruitment Consultants

Advertised vacancies account for approximately 25 per cent of positions filled. The recruitment consultant's role differs from that of the headhunter in that he uses the advertised recruitment process, sometimes referred to as *selection* to provide his client with a shortlist of applicants.

Recruitment consultants may vary from those handling specific industries or professions to those handling the entire scene, but their approach is still very much the same. After taking a brief from their client, they may undertake the whole recruitment process themselves, which will include advertising under their own name, selecting a preliminary list of candidates, applying selection tests of various types, interviewing and finally submitting a shortlist of applicants to their client. Alternatively, the consultant may only deal with part of the recruitment process, for example placing the advertisement and handling the response with all applications being then forwarded to their client. The skill of the recruitment consultant lies in taking an accurate brief from their client, preparing a detailed job description and recruitment specification, creating an imaginative advertisement and advising the client on the most appropriate media to use.

These days very few selection consultants keep a database of applicants. They receive hundreds of applications in response to any advertisement they place, suggesting there is hardly a shortage of applicants. When they undertake a fresh assignment for a similar position, it is not really worth their while wading through several thousand applications, so they place another advertisement in the newspaper. At least this way, they can be sure they are providing their client with up-to-date applications. Experience has shown selection consultants that retaining and maintaining a database of applicants is not really practical, because few people take the trouble to keep them aware of changes in their career or ask to be removed from the database. Consequently a database is often out of date at any one point in time.

You would be best advised to establish whether sending your CV on a speculative basis would be welcomed by search consultants. One way of doing this is to use a publication such as the *CEPEC Recruitment Guide* that not only tells you whether speculative applications are accepted, but provides you with a contact name to whom your CV can be addressed.

### Recruitment Agencies

You may be thinking that recruitment agencies only deal in temporary vacancies, but this is certainly not the case; there are now many agencies specialising in permanent positions for specific industries and businesses. Perhaps the best source for locating recruitment agencies is *Yellow Pages* and a wide selection of these are available at your local library. If you have any doubt about the ability of an agency to help you with your job search I would recommend that you telephone them first before sending your CV.

### Fees

Headhunters, recruitment consultants and recruitment agencies do not charge you a fee for their services. In all cases the fee is paid by the employer.

## Outplacement Services

### Corporate Outplacement Services

Headhunters, recruitment consultants and recruitment agencies are not the only organisations that can play a part in a person leaving one job and gaining another. Outplacement organisations also have a major role to play, for example in helping clients to clarify career direction and to identify their strengths and potential.

Outplacement organisations exist to help individuals find new jobs. They do not secure positions, but provide services that empower individuals to win jobs. The fees of outplacement organisations are normally paid by the individual's current or most recent employer. Whereas recruitment organisations work on behalf of the future employer looking for staff, outplacement organisations work with the individual job-seeker on behalf of the previous employer. Consequently, an employer wanting to release some of its management or staff will seek outplacement services, while an employer seeking to engage management or staff will employ a recruitment organisation.

## Retail Outplacement Services

Some outplacement companies also undertake work for individuals who pay their own fees – this is known as retail outplacement.

A word of caution is necessary if you are thinking about using some of your redundancy settlement to buy outplacement services. Most people who lose their job through redundancy experience stress and a loss of confidence and therefore may not be ideally placed to look around for the best outplacement services or the best deal. Standards in retail outplacement vary considerably, for example in the area of counselling, where the expertise and background of consultants may vary considerably. Other concerns would include the nature of the services provided, their cost and the time limits for these services.

Truly professional retail outplacement services will include career advice, help with self-marketing and counselling from properly trained experts that can get to the heart of a person's hopes, ambitions, life, strengths and potential.

# Jobcentres

This is a free service, provided by the government to help organisations publicise their vacancies to those people interested in a new job. The Jobcentres aim to provide a service to all people looking for employment, whether they are in work or not. They also provide help for the long-term unemployed. Jobcentres operate by displaying vacancies on their noticeboards, enabling visitors to browse through the details before making further enquiries that are dealt with by a client adviser.

The client adviser will draw up a back-to-work plan and tell you about other services available that include job search seminars, job review workshops and the Restart course. The Employment Service has also set up Executive JobClubs in cities and major towns. If you have been unemployed for six months or longer, you are eligible to join one of these clubs. The benefits of JobClubs are that they provide free use of telephones, typewriters, photocopiers, stationery, postage stamps, newspapers and journals. Some help is also available in meeting the costs of travelling to interviews. The JobClub leader also offers advice and support.

## Computerised Registers

A much more recent development is that of candidate registers available through systems such as the Internet. This fast-growing global network of 30 million computer users includes government departments, universities, large and small businesses who use it for worldwide communication and to access thousands of libraries and databases. Organisations have formed an employment network and invite people to register, usually free of charge. Employers who pay a fee and subscribe to the network can then access the candidate database via their desk-top terminals. If they find a candidate who matches their criteria, they can contact the candidate direct or if you have asked for your details to be kept confidential, the company managing the employment network would do so on behalf of the employer.

Usually, the company managing the employment network will supply their own form as a standard CV format. Clearly, there are disadvantages to this, since space will be limited. If you choose to register, you must therefore think very carefully about what to include on their form. If you are contacted by an employer direct or via the employment network, then be prepared to 'sell yourself', but also make sure that you ask enough questions to provide you with adequate information about the company and the job before you commit yourself to the next stage.

This may well become a popular way of accessing candidate information for some employers. However, any system like this relies very heavily on being up-to-date. Nothing will frustrate an employer more than contacting six candidates, only to find that five of them are no longer in the employment market. So if you do choose to register then keep the network aware of any changes in your circumstances.

## Exhibitions

Some employers find a useful form of recruitment is to hire a stand at one of the many recruitment exhibitions held across the country. For those seeking work in a specific industry – for example, financial sales, information technology, hotels and health care – they can often provide a great deal of information.

To find out more about exhibitions, try obtaining a booklet called *Exhibition Bulletin*, published monthly by the London Bureau. Before paying for this booklet, ask at your local library, who may obtain a copy for you free of charge.

## TV and Radio

Some employers (those with a healthy recruitment advertising budget) advertise vacancies through Teletext and on local radio.

## Professional Associations

If you are a member of a professional association, you may find that they offer a service to their members that includes the carrying of brief job advertisements in their newsletters. Whilst this is often a goodwill gesture on the part of your association, it should not be discounted as yet another source of vacancies.

## Networking

Networking in job search terms enables you to draw up a list of useful people – not just friends, but people you have met at some point in your career. A carefully crafted letter is sent to each person on your list requesting a short meeting at which you will ask for their advice and the names of other contacts for you to meet. The aim of these meetings is to locate appropriate job opportunities, a strategy which often works.

Because this is such an important strategy in your job search plan, Chapter 10 – The Art of Networking, is dedicated to this subject.

# 10

# The Art of Networking

*'A modest man is often admired – If people ever hear of him'*
E. W. Howe

## What is Networking?

Networking is about making the most of your contacts. In the world of recruitment there are many people who put a high value on a strong recommendation from a reliable source, rather than going through the sometimes lengthy and expensive business of advertising and processing a large number of application forms. Making the most of your contacts is exploiting this well-known pointer towards finding your next job.

Networking involves drawing up a list of suitable contacts and approaching them. At your meeting, the aim is to get your initial contacts to provide you with more contacts. You meet the second layer of contacts who should again provide you with yet more contacts and so it goes on. As in any other form of networking, this cascading approach very quickly expands your list of contacts.

Meeting up with your contacts in this way has nothing to do with directly approaching employers for jobs. If it were, you could be sure that your supply of contacts would very quickly dry up. Try putting yourself in the position of someone who receives hundreds of unsolicited CVs and job enquiries. On top of this, someone who claims they met up with you whilst attending a recent training course telephones to see if he could come and see you to discuss career opportunities with your company. Need I say more? The outcome of this sort of enquiry is predictable. Most will get a polite 'I'm sorry, my diary is very full at the moment'. For the few who manage to arrange a meeting, this will probably turn out to be a rather embarrassing one-sided encounter. Contacts approached in this way will certainly not provide you with further names for your list, they value their own reputation too greatly.

## The Correct Networking Technique

As I have explained, if a contact is approached in the wrong way, they will feel cornered and possibly under threat. So you may ask, if I don't use the direct approach, how can it possibly lead to my getting a new job? Networking needs a much more subtle technique. For example, flattering your contacts with a statement about their knowledge of the industry and then asking for a short meeting of say 15-20 minutes to pick their brains for advice and guidance will almost certainly work and lead to yet more contacts. Ultimately the aim of networking is of course not to provide you with a never-ending list of contacts. Somewhere along the line, during one of your contact meetings, you will encounter someone with the right vacancy and you will generate sufficient interest in your background and experience for them to offer you this position.

## Networking Letters

Begin by drawing up a list of four or five initial contacts. Those on the initial list should ideally be business people holding positions of influence, whom you have known for some time. They need not be close friends, in fact this often makes matters worse because a meeting under these circumstances can quite often place a strain on any friendship.

Writing to a list of contacts is much better than telephoning, although there is nothing wrong with writing first and then following this up with a telephone call. Of course you don't send your CV with your letter.

Below is a suggested format for a typical networking letter, but do make use of your own ideas:

---

Your address

Mr David Palmer
Group Finance Director
ABC Engineering Technology Ltd
Shipham Industrial Estate
LIVERPOOL L63 8BT

Date

Dear David,

As you have probably read in the press recently, Midland Engineering has been taken over by the Amalgamated Metals Group. The new company have decided to handle management accounting within the existing Group, so my job together with those of my ten staff will disappear at the end of this month.

I am not writing to ask you for a job, but in view of your knowledge of the industry, I do believe I would benefit from some of your expert advice and guidance before I plan my next move.

Could you check your diary to see if you could fit me in for a short meeting of say 15 minutes? If it is convenient, I will telephone your secretary in a few days' time to arrange this.

Kind regards.

Your sincerely

## Networking Meetings

Never force the pace during this meeting, but do try to maintain control. Begin by confirming the information in your letter, but do not dwell on this for too long as it can often sound rather negative. Explain that you are looking for help in putting together your job-search plan and keep your sights on the objective. Remember, your aim is to come away with a handful of further contact names.

After your contact meeting, always send a follow-up letter. This is not just a matter of courtesy, but it sends out the right signals, creating a good and lasting impression. Your contact is much more inclined to remember you and to maintain an interest in your next round of meetings. Again, I have provided you with a suggested format for this type of letter opposite.

## The Art of Networking

> Your address
>
> Mr David Palmer
> Group Finance Director
> ABC Engineering Technology Ltd
> Shipham Industrial Estate
> LIVERPOOL L63 8BT
>
> Date
>
> Dear David,
>
> It was good to meet up with you yesterday, thank you for your advice and guidance. I appreciate that this is a particularly busy time of the year for your company and yet you were kind enough to spare me more than an hour of your time.
>
> I have written today to John Dickens of Worthington Steel Parts and of course I will keep you informed of developments. Whatever the outcome, I am very grateful for your generous help.
>
> Yours sincerely

Once John Dickens of Worthington Steel Parts receives your letter he should be receptive to your request for a meeting – after all, you were recommended by his golfing colleague, David Palmer.

To summarise then: networking can be an extremely powerful tool in the job-search toolkit if used correctly and with enthusiasm.

*Manage Your Career*

PERSONNEL MANAGER: "FOR THIS JOB WE NEED SOMEONE WHO IS RESPONSIBLE."

APPLICANT: "THAT'S ME, AT MY LAST JOB, WHENEVER ANYTHING WENT WRONG, THEY ALWAYS SAID I WAS RESPONSIBLE."

# 11
# Responding to Advertised Vacancies

*Seen in the employment section of a local newspaper:*
*'Position requires wisdom of Solomon, patience of Job, skill*
*of David. No other applicants have a prayer.'*

As we have already said in an earlier chapter, job advertisements can be found in the classified pages of national newspapers, local newspapers and professional and trade magazines, journals and newsletters. I have listed the most important national newspapers which carry job advertisements in Chapters 9 and 17. Don't feel you have to buy these papers regularly because they are available within your local library.

Much advice about locating job advertisements has been included in Chapter 9. However in this chapter we shall concentrate on how to respond to your chosen job advertisement.

## What to Look For in Advertisements

When you scan the advertisement columns your first priority will probably be job title and salary, but do check everything carefully. Job titles can vary between organisations as indeed can the content of jobs with the same job title.

If you find an advertisement of interest, then your next step should be to study the advertisement further, word for word. Job adverts generally have three separate areas: a description of the company, details of the role or job to be done and the skills and experience requirements of the person sought, together with information about salary and benefits and how to apply. Some advertisements are clear and very well-written, particularly those placed by the better selection consultants. However there are also many which are badly written and tell you very little about the advertiser's requirements.

When you're studying an advertisement try asking yourself the following questions:

- What type and size of company is this?
- What does this job involve?
- What are the responsibilities?
- What qualifications do they require?
- What experience are they looking for?
- What skills do they need?
- What other qualities do they ask for?
- What is the age range?
- What is the salary?
- Where is the job based?

What you are looking for are those words which help you identify the advertiser's job requirements. One useful technique is to underline or highlight each of these words on the advertisement and then to transfer these words on to a separate sheet of paper.

Now try to look for clues which will help you determine the level of importance to attach to each requirement, and then rank them further down your sheet of paper.

Put yourself in the employer's position – you are trying to attract the best possible applicant for the job. Quite often the advert is designed to rule out those applicants who do not meet the requirements of their job specification and employee specification. However, for some employers, the ideal candidate described in the advert probably doesn't exist.

If you have your list of ranked requirements and you match 60 per cent or more of these, then go ahead and apply. If you match less than 60 per cent, you must be guided by the level of importance of each requirement, and which of your own skills can be matched with these.

Clearly if you cannot match with the employer's number one or two requirements the risk of rejection by the employer is very high. However, if you can gear yourself to receiving lots of rejection letters then I would recommend that you should apply despite this hurdle.

## Ageism

If an employer mentions an age limit in their advertisement, try not to be put off by this. Whilst some employers apply these limits strictly, others recognise that such limits are for the ideal applicant. When faced with an applicant who satisfies all their requirements except that of age they will often be prepared to offer that applicant an interview. Only if you are well outside an age limit should you refer to this in your covering letter. Putting it across in a positive way, for example by reinforcing the depth of your experience, will be more to your advantage than simply leaving it for the employer to discover.

## Other Points to Look For

It is essential that you fully comply with any instructions the advert provides on how to apply. These may include:

- *Please send a covering letter with your CV*
- *Please telephone for an application form*
- *Please call or send your career details quoting the following ref No*
- *To apply for this vacancy please send a full CV accompanied by a letter outlining the reasons why you would be suitable for the position*
- *Write with full career and salary details*
- *To apply please write with your CV detailing particularly any experience in . . .*
- *In the first instance please telephone the following number for an exploratory discussion . . .*

Whilst you may feel tempted, don't use the fax unless you are specifically asked to do so and then always follow up with a hard copy.

## Application Letters

Many job advertisements ask you to forward a CV together with a covering letter. It is important to produce this to the same professional standard as your CV. What is the point in producing a really good CV if you send it with a letter that simply states 'As you requested in your advertisement, I am enclosing a copy of my CV'? Just as bad are those letters which contain grammatical mistakes, typing errors and poor presentation.

The real drawback, even with a good CV, is the general nature of its content. Ideally you should personalise your CV for every application, but this really is a cumbersome approach, particularly taking into account the volume of your applications. You must always provide a covering letter so why not take the opportunity to address the company's requirements within the advertisement by matching these with your own skills and experience? This is a very effective way of personalising your application for any specific vacancy.

Unless you are asked to supply a handwritten letter, which sometimes means your handwriting will be studied by a graphologist, you should aim to provide a typed letter to the same standard as your CV. Use the same typeface or font and use the same quality paper.

To show how all the points so far can be used in the production of a suitable covering letter, study the advertisement on the following page. Underline what you consider to be the important words or phrases which help to spell out the employer's requirements.

## Regional Sales Manager
**Outstanding Career Opportunity**
**North West • Circa £35,000 + Bonus + Quality Car**

We are part of a substantial, long established organisation embarking on an exciting new phase of development through the major re-launch of an exceptional range of benefits and services. Customer focused, we are firmly set to capitalise on our unrivalled position and can offer this outstanding opportunity to an accomplished Sales Manager.

With full responsibility for sales operations in the North West of England, you will lead and direct the field sales force. This will involve setting targets, recruiting and training in line with our expansion programme, implementing sales initiatives and generally managing performance levels within the North West. Reporting to the Sales Director you will be a full member of the national sales management team determining the future shape and success of the company.

This is an extremely high profile role. To succeed you will need to demonstrate success in a results orientated sales environment where your motivational and leadership skills ensured targets were regularly surpassed.

In return, a basic salary of £35k is offered plus a generous bonus and a quality car.

Please send a comprehensive CV with covering letter and current salary details, quoting ref: RA6 to **David Jones, Human Resource Director** at the following address:

**A N Other Engineering plc
230 Black & White Lane
Guildford
Surrey SU3 1DL**

## Responding to Advertised Vacancies

When you have underlined all the relevant words and phrases in this typical if rather wordy advertisement, your list should contain all of the following:

- ✓ Long established organisation
- ✓ New phase of development
- ✓ Major re-launch of benefits and services
- ✓ Customer focused
- ✓ Full responsibility for sales operations
- ✓ Lead and direct the sales force
- ✓ Setting targets
- ✓ Recruiting and training
- ✓ Implementing sales initiatives
- ✓ Generally managing performance
- ✓ Demonstrate success in a results orientated sales environment
- ✓ Motivational and leadership skills
- ✓ Ensuring targets were surpassed

Whilst the first three items in this list are not really requirements, they have been included because they tell you something about the company and the nature of the job.

The next step is to rank the remaining ten requirements in what you consider to be the order of their priority to the company:

1. Full responsibility for sales operations
2. Demonstrate success in a results orientated sales environment
   Ensuring targets were surpassed
   Setting targets

3. Motivational and leadership skills
   Generally managing performance
   Recruiting and training
   Implementing sales initiatives
   Lead and direct the sales force
4. Customer focused

In my opinion this company places *'full responsibility for sales operations'* as probably encompassing all the other requirements which follow, so for that reason it has been placed at number 1 on our list. Further careful study of the list has enabled some of the requirements to be placed into groups of the same or similar requirements. For example, group 2 is all about experience of the setting and achievement of sales targets. Group 3 amounts to a list of man-management skills. Finally, *'Customer focused'* has been placed at number 4 because although it is used more often as a description of the company, all applicants would be wise to regard it as important indicator of the style of management required.

Once the employer's requirements have been ranked, you can set about the business of trying to match your own skills against these. In this case we are going to assume that the applicant does indeed have a good match with the employer's requirements. Based on this assumption I have illustrated several examples of a covering letter to accompany an application form.

## Responding to Advertised Vacancies

## Example 1

```
0161 820 000                          26 Marine Avenue
                                      Bookwood
                                      Manchester

                                      Date


Mr David Jones
Human Resource Director
A N Other Engineering plc
230 Black & White Lane
Guildford
Surrey SU3 1DL


Ref RA6

Dear David,
I was very interested in your ad in the sunday times for a Sales
Manager and would like to be considered for this interesting post.
As you will see from my cv, I have lots of sales experience gained
from working for a number of employers and I am particularly well
versed in customer care techniques.
I have always acheived good results and respect from the men who
have worked for me and I have never let my employers down.I have
excellent management skills and would look forward to being a full
member of your national sale management team.
I am available at any time to be interviewed.
Yours faithfully


*A. Candidate*
```

119

Frankly, there's not a great deal to commend this candidate to the recruiter. Here are a list of my comments:

- ✗ He begins by addressing the HR Director by his Christian name. Although the HR Director has used his Christian name in the advertisement, you must not assume, unless this person is a colleague of yours, that it is correct to use it in your covering letter.
- ✗ There is no reference to which dated issue of the *Sunday Times* the advertisement appeared.
- ✗ Why should the employer plod through the CV to see the extent of this applicant's sales experience? The reference to a number of employers might also suggest to some recruiters that there is a lack of stability in this person's employment record. He has also misread the relative importance of customer care as being worthy of comment.
- ✗ In general he seems to expect the recruiter to accept everything he says on face value as no specific achievements are mentioned.
- ✗ There is a too frequent use of the word 'I'.
- ✗ There are some basic grammatical mistakes:

Shortening of advertisement to 'ad'.
The use of lower case in *Sunday Times* and CV.
Missing 's' from sales.

- ✗ Presentation leaves a lot to be desired:

Is this a telephone number in the top left hand corner of the letter?
Where is the applicant's postcode?
Layout is inconsistent in the applicant's address and recruiter's address.

## Responding to Advertised Vacancies

There is a gap at the beginning of the second paragraph with no gap after the first sentence in the third paragraph.
- ✗ Misspelling of achieved.
- ✗ The applicant has not followed the instructions in the advertisement as there is no reference to his salary.
- ✗ Incorrect use of *Yours faithfully*. This should not be used when addressing someone by name.
- ✗ Rather than struggle to read the applicant's signature, it would be sensible to print the name after the signature.

In conclusion, this is a most unsatisfactory covering letter that creates a very poor image in the eyes of the recruiter. You may be appalled at the standard of this letter, but unfortunately such letters are all too often received by recruiters. This one is destined to end up in the 'NO' pile, shortly to be followed by the shredder!

## Example 2

Tel: 0161 820 000

26 Marine Avenue
Bookwood
Manchester
M65 9TT

Date

Mr David Jones
Human Resource Director
A N Other Engineering plc
230 Black & White Lane
Guildford
Surrey SU3 1DL

Dear Mr Jones,

*Ref: RA6 – Sales Manager*

Please accept this application for the above appointment, which was advertised in the Sunday Times on 10 July 1995.

As you will see from the attached CV, I can offer the following relevant background and experience:

- 15 years' sales experience, achieving my first sales management position with full responsibility for all sales operations 5 years ago.
- Throughout my career I have frequently achieved performance standards in excess of sales targets within a customer focused growth industry.
- As a Sales Manager I have set sales targets and contributed to the company's business plans. In the last two years, my sales team received awards for the best performance against budget in the company.
- Responsible for the recruitment, training and development of a team of 15 sales representatives. This has included the delivery of specific training courses and recognition by the company of my strong coaching skills.

My current salary details are £32k basic salary plus a bonus payment which has averaged a further £5k in the last 12 months.

I am confident that you will find these details are a good match for the requirements contained in your advertisement and look forward to hearing from you.

Yours sincerely

*B. Applicant*

B. Applicant

## Responding to Advertised Vacancies

The contrast between Example 2 and Example 1 couldn't be greater. What is good about Example 2?:

- ✓ The applicant clearly sets out where and when he saw the advertisement.
- ✓ Emphasises the key elements of his background, experience and achievements which match the recruiter's requirements.
- ✓ Fully complies with the recruiter's instructions in the advertisement.
- ✓ The presentation is good.

Another style you can use when preparing a covering letter has come to be known as the executive briefing. Quite simply you provide a list of the company's requirements on the left side of your letter and your skills and experience, matching point by point the company's requirements, on the right. This has become particularly popular with recruitment specialists because it enables them to quickly determine whether you are suitable for interview. There is an example of this style on the following page.

## Example 3

Tel: 0161 820 000

26 Marine Avenue
Bookwood
Manchester
M65 9TT

Date

Mr David Jones
Human Resource Director
A N Other Engineering plc
230 Black & White Lane
Guildford
Surrey SU3 1DL

Dear Mr Jones,

Ref: RA6 – Sales Manager

Please accept this application for the above appointment, which was advertised in the Sunday Times on 10 July 1995.

Whilst I have enclosed, as requested, a copy of my CV which will provide you with a general outline of my experience to date and some of my achievements, I have taken the opportunity to list below your current requirements for this post and my applicable skills in those areas.

| Your requirements | My skills and experience |
|---|---|
| Full responsibility for sales operations. | 15 years' sales experience, the last 5 years as Sales Manager with responsibility for all sales operations. |
| Generally managing performance. Success in a results orientated sales environment. Setting targets and ensuring they are surpassed. | Frequently achieved performance standards in excess of sales targets. Set sales targets and contributed to businessplans. My sales team received awards for the best performance against budget. |
| Recruitment and Training. Motivational and leadership skills. | Responsible for recruitment and training of 15 sales representatives. Delivering training courses and coaching. |

My current salary details are £32k basic salary plus a bonus payment which has averaged a further £5k in the last 12 months.

I am confident that you will find these details are a good match for your requirements and look forward to hearing from you.

Yours sincerely

*C. Applicant*

C. Applicant

Remember, these are only examples of a well-written letter. Don't attempt to copy them when you are writing your own covering letters; try instead to build up your own list of suitable phrases and terms.

Always use a quality A4-size envelope for your CV and accompanying letter and use a first-class stamp – the small difference in cost between first- and second-class post is well worth it to make sure that your valuable application arrives in good time.

## Application Forms

Earlier in this chapter we reviewed different ways in which employers ask applicants to respond to their advertisements. From an applicant's viewpoint, the least popular style is to telephone or write for an application form. Why is this so unpopular? Well first and foremost, who amongst us actually enjoys filling in forms of any sort? They are a test of not only your handwriting but also your ability to reduce a group of words into the optimum number which will fit into those all-too-often ridiculously small boxes provided on the form.

Whilst application forms do serve a useful purpose to employers, they are really best kept until the first screening for interview stage has been completed. At this point, when you know you have been selected for interview, being asked to complete an application form seems to have more of a purpose.

Application forms often run from one to about six pages in length. The format is usually one of factual information about your education and training, career, health and interests. There is also between a half to one page of white space in which you are asked questions about reasons for applying for the job, your career aspirations and the contribution you think you can make.

Here are some useful tips to consider before completing application forms:

- Begin by taking a photocopy of the form. Check content, spelling and grammar on the copy before completing the original.
- Always read through the form and any accompanying notes carefully.
- Writing application forms rather than typing them is best, since trying to type into those small boxes with any degree of accuracy is difficult and prone to error. Always work on the photocopied form and fill this in before attempting to complete the original.
- Always follow any instructions given. For example, you may be asked to complete the form in black ink or to use block capitals.
- Response to factual questions is straightforward, but those which are open-ended should be drafted and redrafted until you are satisfied with your response. Refer to your CV and the information you have built up during your reading of Chapter 5: The Importance of Knowing Yourself, and bring your achievements, strengths and skills into full use. The technique in responding to these questions is to try and match the information you provide with the requirements in the employer's advertisement or job and employee specification, just as you did with your CV and covering letter. If you can spare some time to carry out focused research on the company, then use words or expressions that show you know something about them.
- Choose each word carefully, and as a general rule stick to the space provided, even if you are invited to use a continuation sheet. Many employers design their forms to

## Responding to Advertised Vacancies

provide what they consider to be enough space to answer these questions. If you insist on using a continuation sheet, you are probably adopting an over-wordy approach which will have less impact on the reader.

- If there are gaps in your application, perhaps because of time out for study, to travel or to look after your family, then give an account of them on the form. If you don't, they will raise questions in the mind of the recruiter and undermine your application.
- Just as with your CV, never include any negative information in the application form, but rather adopt a positive approach.
- Should you include a copy of your CV? Yes, but never write 'See CV' in answer to any questions on the application form.
- When you are satisfied with your draft, go on to carefully complete the original copy of the form. Return the form to the employer with a covering letter following the same set of rules and sample letter to be found earlier in this chapter. Post back the form using a first-class stamp.
- Some application forms ask for referees. Before providing this information, make sure you have their permission to do so.
- Keep a copy of the form for reference purposes; you will find this helpful if you are invited for interview.

# 12

# Making Speculative Applications

*'Let him that would move the world,
first move himself'*

Socrates

Earlier references have been made to that part of the job market sometimes called the 'hidden market' which includes recruitment specialists such as headhunters and recruitment consultants. Headhunters in particular do not advertise on behalf of their clients and whilst recruitment consultants do advertise, some also provide search facilities for their clients, using a database of candidates. The technique of networking has also been shown to be an effective means of locating jobs which may not be advertised.

In this chapter we shall be taking a closer look at how best to approach this rich source of job vacancies.

## *Speculative Letters to Recruitment Specialists*

Assuming you have identified the recruitment specialists you will be approaching, then the next step is to send each of them a copy of your CV with an appropriate covering letter. Here are the ground rules to follow in each and every case:

- Identify the name, initials and title of the person who deals with speculative enquiries.
- There is no reason why the content of these letters should not be identical or similar providing they *look individual*.
- Draft and redraft your letter until you are satisfied with the content, keeping this to one side of an A4 sheet.
- As with letters responding to advertised vacancies, make sure your letters are free from mistakes of any kind and that the layout is always neat.
- It is preferable to type these letters, using good quality A4 paper and envelopes.
- Always try to create the very best impression.
- Use first-class postage stamps.

On the following page is a sample speculative letter to a recruitment specialist.

## Making Speculative Applications

## *Sample speculative letter to a recruitment specialist*

Tel: 0161 820 000

26 Marine Avenue
Bookwood
Manchester
M90 3BT

Date

Mr Peter Hall
Senior Consultant
XYZ Consultants
Park Road
Manchester
M6 3HH

Dear Mr Hall,

I am a Sales Manager with considerable experience in the fmcg market and am seeking a new appointment.

Whilst I would be particularly interested in sales management appointments, I am currently reviewing my career to date and see this as an ideal opportunity to extend my general management skills.

My current salary consists of £32,000 pa basic salary, an annual bonus of approximately £5,000 plus fully expensed car and private medical insurance. I would be willing to relocate within the UK for the right position.

I should be grateful if you would consider me for any relevant assignments and would welcome any advice you can provide. I enclose a copy of my CV and look forward to hearing from you.

Yours sincerely

## Speculative Letters to Employers

Sending speculative letters to employers can be a useful part of your job-search strategy. However there are certain ground rules to follow to make this type of approach worthwhile. The first rule is to conduct some focused research to determine the most suitable employers to approach. All the assistance you need to conduct this research is given in Chapter 7: Researching the Job Market. The second rule is to use your research findings to create truly individual letters.

Employers receive a great many unsolicited job applications and with a few exceptions, most will only give these a cursory glance before passing them on to their personnel manager for a polite *no thank you* letter.

If your speculative letter is to stand any chance of being fully read and actioned, the content must contain something which gets the reader's attention immediately, and at this point I'm not talking about your skills!

The purpose of your focused research is to try and unearth something worthwhile about the company to whom you are writing. Some examples might include:

- Development or introduction of new products or services
- The opening of a new factory or offices
- Success in a particular field
- The acquisition of other companies
- An award of BS5750 or training awards etc.

Some of the sources quoted in Chapter 7 will help you narrow down the information you want. I would also suggest telephoning the company and asking for a copy of their annual report or annual staff report – these are usually produced by the company's public relations department. Start your letter by stating in which newspaper, magazine or report you read about the company and what you found of interest. The next tip is to find a way of linking this to your background and experience, whilst offering your services. What you are demonstrating by this approach is that you are interested in the company and that you have done your homework.

The third rule is to address your letter to the right person by name and job title. If you are thinking of writing to the personnel manager of a company, then there are a few drawbacks. This person may only know about current vacancies and not those that are, for whatever reason, still at the planning stage. You might well receive a more enthusiastic response if you address your letter to the director responsible for the part of the business where you could be employed or alternatively you could try addressing your letter to the managing director.

On the following page is a sample speculative letter to an employer.

*Manage Your Career*

# Sample speculative letter to an employer

Tel: 0161 820 000                        26 Marine Avenue
Bookwood
Manchester
M90 3BT

Date

Mr P A Bell
Sales Director
Green & Brown plc
Manchester
M60 8XX

Dear Mr Bell

I recently came across a most interesting article in the *Sunday Times* describing the success and growth of your company. Your announcement to open a new sales office in South Manchester was of particular interest and as someone with a strong and successful sales background I am writing to enquire if there may also be new sales opportunities where my experience could make a profitable contribution.

Throughout my 15 years' experience of sales, I have frequently achieved performance standards in excess of sales targets. As a Sales Manager for the last five years, I have significantly increased the North West sales performance for my current employer and negotiated contracts with key customers.

A copy of my CV is enclosed and I would welcome a meeting to discuss potential vacancies in your new Manchester sales office and my experience and achievements in greater detail.

I look forward to hearing from you.

Yours sincerely

## Making Speculative Applications

This speculative letter has a lot to commend it since it starts with something to grab the reader's attention and then moves straight into a no-nonsense *I have something to offer – are you interested?* approach.

Just as with all job-search letters, speculative letters to employers should be kept to one side of an A4 sheet, there must be no mistakes and the layout must be neat. Preferably type the letter and use good quality paper and envelopes.

# 13

# Winning at Interviews

*'We judge ourselves by what we feel capable of doing; others judge us by what we have done'*
Henry Wadsworth Longfellow

So you have achieved your goal and secured an interview. What happens now? Well, never take this stage in the recruitment process for granted. There is much to learn and a great deal of preparation to undertake before you set off for your interview.

The business of job interviews is not a science and is carried out badly by some employers, despite their good intentions. Whilst some personnel and human resources people and even fewer line managers have received training in interview technique, it has to be said that the interview as a selection technique has changed very little in the last 50 years. The outcome is that you, the applicant should expect varying standards when called for interview.

## Interviews with Consultants

Many employers use recruitment specialists to help them recruit for a wide range of jobs. Their role is fully explained in Chapter 9: Vacancies – How and Where to Find Them. You can expect a recruitment specialist to be thorough and professional from his first meeting with the client to the final interview – this is how he earns his fee from the client.

You will probably hear about a job from a recruitment consultant in one of the following ways:

- You have received a telephone call from a headhunter. His assignment is to track down likely candidates who fit his client's specification so the post will not have been advertised. He may check the information he holds about your background and experience and will then arrange an interview.
- You have responded to an advertisement placed by a recruitment consultant on behalf of his client and have been selected for interview.
- You have sent your CV on a speculative basis to a recruitment consultant and have been sent a job description for an assignment they are currently handling. Following a brief telephone conversation with the recruitment consultant to clarify certain aspects of the role and your experience, the consultant has invited you for an interview.

Having been invited for interview, it's important to recognise that all recruitment specialists vary in the amount of information they give you about the job and their client prior to the interview. If the post has not been advertised, they will probably not disclose the name of their client and even if the post has been advertised this information may still be withheld. In some cases, you may be told the name of the client during the interview, but this will not help you with the sort of preparation that is strongly recommended before any job interview.

The typical length of an interview with a recruitment specialist is in excess of one hour and often follows a rather different form from an interview with an employer. The first point to make is that if you do know the name of the client, a recruitment specialist will not expect you to have prepared in quite the same way you would have done before an interview with an employer. Often the interview will start with a description of the client and the job, during which time you will be invited to ask questions. This will be followed by questions based on the needs of the client company and how your background, skills and experience might match them. Finally, the interview will conclude with a discussion of your career and personal needs and how closely the company and the reward package might meet them. I can't promise you that every recruitment specialist will follow this routine; some may well launch straight into questions about your career and experience. Whatever their style, my advice is to go along with it. This person represents the client so your aim must be to create the best impression.

This type of interview is usually conducted in informal surroundings, more than likely with soft, comfortable chairs and only a coffee table between yourself and the interviewer. Don't be taken in too much by this informality. It's fatal to over-relax and assume the questions will be equally low-pitched. The chances are the questions will be put across in a friendly fashion but they will be nonetheless searching. So keep your wits about you throughout the interview.

Most of the questions you will be asked will relate to your level of competence, through a detailed evaluation of your CV. You will also be asked your management style, with questions to elicit your views and opinions on a range of subjects that will enable the interviewer to form an opinion of your acceptability to the client, and how you might relate to the culture of the company.

This type of interviewer is very experienced and will usually spot inflated claims, so you are best always giving honest answers and avoiding a waffling response. Present yourself in the most positive and favourable light. Be positive about your career progression so far and what you have achieved. Be equally positive and enthusiastic about your next move and what this company will gain from offering you the job. This structure is one favoured by recruitment specialists who will rule you out all too quickly if you put across a negative attitude. If there are any negative events in your career, then stress that these were brought about by external circumstances and were not within your span of control.

Prepare yourself by reflecting on your CV and put yourself in the role of the interviewer. Prepare a list of demanding questions based on the content of your CV and make sure you can answer them competently.

If the interviewer hasn't given you adequate information about the job at the beginning of the interview, he will usually allow some time at the end for your questions or for you to make any additional points in support of your application. Put across the experience and achievements that you think are relevant, but keep it brief. Ask about the company and the job but again restrict your questions to those which help you to form a picture of what this company is like to work for.

The interviewer will probably close the interview by giving you information about the next stage in the selection process and the likely timescale. If he doesn't, then don't be afraid to ask.

## Interviews with Employers

Employers apply various standards to the selection interview, but they generally fall into one of the following categories:

- An explanatory interview by a line manager or personnel representative. Quite often this approach is used if the employer has advertised an 'open day' for applicants to find out more about the employer and the advertised vacancies. Usually held away from company premises in informal surroundings.
- Interviews by one or more line managers.
- Interviews by one or more line managers and invited back for a second interview usually with a senior line manager.
- Interviews by one or more line managers and a representative from the personnel department.
- **Sequential interviews**

    The first interview is usually with a representative from the personnel department followed by a second interview with one or more line managers at which a representative from personnel may be present. This is often not a satisfactory selection technique and could suggest an organisation that has not adequately delegated the authority to recruit to its line managers.
- **Interviews by a panel or selection board**

    Interview panels usually have two or three people whilst a selection board is a larger, more formal interviewing process often used in the public sector. From the applicant's viewpoint, questions often seem unplanned and to be delivered at random. This type of interview can be very stressful for some applicants.

- **Stress interviews**
  This type of interview is rare, but some companies, particularly those recruiting well-paid sales jobs, still ask applicants to attend these interviews. The technique is based on applying various pressures to determine how well you will stand up to pressures in the actual job. The whole stance is tough and unbending, with interviewers criticising or questioning your judgement and approach.
- **Group interviews**
  This involves getting a number of candidates together with observers from the company. The objective is to see how applicants interact with each other. The general procedure involves one of the company observers providing the group with a case study that includes features and problems similar to those they would meet if they joined the company. They may also be asked to discuss a general social or economic problem. The observers then note who makes a contribution, if the contribution is constructive or negative, who leads or dominates the discussion, who strays off the point, who keeps quiet etc. Observers often ask candidates to take turns in leading the group. This tests for leadership qualities and finely tunes the observers' own views and opinions of the candidates. Lunch is often provided and should be seen as a continuation of the assessment process.
- Interviewed by a headhunter or recruitment specialist and shortlisted for a second interview with a senior line manager or director, at which a senior representative from personnel may be present.

These procedures are unpredictable to say the least and depend very much on the culture of the recruiting organisation, its size and the degree to which personnel and human resources techniques have been applied.

# A Well-Structured Interview

If the company has properly prepared for the interview, they will have begun the process with a job description and an employee specification.

## Job Description

Job descriptions provide basic information about the job under the headings of the job title, reporting relationships, nature and scope of the job and the contribution expected from the job-holder, sometimes called 'principal accountabilities', followed by tasks or duties. Sometimes, as an aid to recruitment, job descriptions also include detail about the competencies required.

## Employee Specification

Employee specifications, sometimes called person, recruitment or personnel specifications, define the knowledge, skills, education, qualifications, special training, experience and personal qualities required by the job-holder. Other information on the special demands made by the job such as unusual hours of work or travel away from home are often included. They may also contain information about terms and conditions of employment.

The employer will take both of these documents to establish a set of assessment criteria against which they can evaluate and record their views of each applicant.

Provided the interview is properly structured, it should not matter if there is one or more than one person conducting the interview. The interviewer's approach will be to try and ensure consistency in the treatment of each applicant. To do this they will identify a set of competencies from the job description based on the technical background, knowledge, career and qualifications necessary for satisfactory performance of the job. They will also identify other competencies that might include:

- Interpersonal skills such as written communication, oral communication, presentation skills, counselling and coaching skills
- Intellectual skills such as analytical reasoning and mental agility
- Commercial skills such as action orientation, project management, commercial drive and commitment to quality

Once these competencies have been identified they can devise suitable questions that seek to establish each applicant's degree of expertise in these areas.

In addition to evaluating the applicant's answers, the interviewer will also be observing the applicant and noting behaviour that adds to the assessment. For example, if oral communication skill is one of the competencies required in the successful candidate, the interviewer might record the following positive and negative observations about several of the applicants:

| | |
|---|---|
| *Positive Observations* | Expresses ideas in a clear, straightforward manner. |
| | Speaks clearly. |
| | Is concise and to the point. |
| | Quick to get and retain my attention. |

| | |
|---|---|
| *Negative observations* | Difficult to follow line of thought.<br>Mumbles and speaks too quickly.<br>Takes a long time to get to the point.<br>Wanders off the topic. |

This approach enables the recruiter to compare candidates much more objectively and removes much of the subjectivity associated with interviews.

## Preparing for your Interview

I cannot overstate the need for adequate preparation for your interview. It has never ceased to amaze me just how many people turn up for interview having put no effort whatsoever into planning or preparation. As a lamb goes to the slaughter, do they really expect the employer to hand over the job if they can't be bothered to show any genuine interest in return? An interview is no different from any other selling process. If you want the employer to sit up and take notice, you have to put across your unique selling points (USPs).

USPs can be divided into two areas of preparation, the first consisting of the background information to the recruiting organisation. Much has been said in earlier chapters about sources of employer information, so there is no need to repeat it. The important point is that once you have been selected for interview, every minute you spend in your local or central library obtaining background information about the company will be well worthwhile. Always telephone the company personnel department and ask for a copy of the job description. You should also ask for a copy of their most recent annual report, staff report or staff magazine and any relevant sales material which can usually be obtained from the personnel department or the PR department. Take another look at the advertisement because you will often find that there are clues there to indicate if the company is expanding or diversifying.

One other avenue with good potential is if the company has shops or showrooms. You could pay them a visit, talk to the receptionist, explain that you have an interview – could they provide you with any useful information?

Study all the information you have gathered and from this compile a résumé of:

- The industry of which this company is a part and the type of problems and issues it is facing
- The company's main area of business
- The company's range of products or services
- Where its main offices or factories are located
- The size of the company in terms of turnover
- How many people work there
- The names of the top senior executives i.e. Chairman, Managing Director
- The company's current plans and problems

What, you may ask, is the purpose of obtaining all this information? To begin with, most applicants go up in the estimation of the employer if they ask for an annual report and sales information. Secondly, you can often relate your own background and experience to the information contained in these reports. Consequently, you may find opportunities to include such information in response to questions from the employer, for example, if you are asked 'What interests you in working for this company?' or 'What do you know about this company?' Even if this type of opportunity doesn't present itself, then there will be other opportunities to include this information when you are invited to ask questions. The point is that using this approach signals to the employer that you are someone who has taken an interest in the company and properly prepared yourself.

To illustrate this point, I recall, during my time as a personnel manager, a young man coming into my office to be interviewed for a job as a sales representative. I asked him what he knew about the company. He said he'd read something about us somewhere. Had he spoken to anyone who worked for the company? No. Had he checked with his local library to see if they had any information about the company? No. All of this left me with one other question. How well prepared would this young man be if he were to call on a prospective customer for us? I already knew the answer.

For the second area of preparation, you need to revisit Chapter 5: The Importance of Knowing Yourself. Take stock of your background, experience, your strengths and weaknesses, your list of transferable skills and personal qualities. If you haven't already carried out a matching exercise between your own list and the employer's requirements found in the advertisement and job description, now is the time to do it. You should also review your CV and covering letter and, if appropriate, the copy you made of the application form.

Armed with this material, you should now set about anticipating the questions you may be asked during the interview and those that you might like to ask.

The most important point to bear in mind is that the employer is using the interview to try and establish how good a match you are for the job requirements. If you are confident that the matching exercise you have carried out has scored highly then be prepared to sell your achievements and – on the basis of what you can do for the employer – your uniqueness. Be prepared to be challenged on what you have said in your CV and try to provide further examples of why this could be of benefit to this employer. Your preparation will increase your confidence, enhance your self-presentation and improve your chance of success. If, during your matching exercise you have identified any areas of weakness, then you will need to rehearse your answers to any potentially difficult questions.

## Prepare to Win

From what you have read in this chapter so far, you will recognise that if you want the job, you have to be prepared to win it. You can always find the time for preparation and practice, particularly if you are unemployed. Practice is very important; it's the factor that can make all the difference. The job market is changing; we can no longer count on one job for life. Instead, a young man leaving university may have to experience as many as ten job changes during his career. The prospect of so many job changes may seem very daunting, but if you're prepared, the pressure is on the others – the ones who haven't done their homework.

## The Interviewer's Questioning Technique

As mentioned earlier, the skill level of those responsible for interviewing can range from competent to poor. Some will take a completely structured approach with well thought-out questions, whilst for others, interviews are an unstructured affair where their questions may seem to have no direct bearing on the job for which you have applied. In some cases interviewers fill the time talking about themselves and the company, or conversely they adopt a passive style expecting you to fill the time talking about yourself without any real guidance. Some interviewers have a relaxed, almost easy-going style whilst others inject more authority into the process. Whatever the competence level of the interviewer or whether the interview is structured or unstructured, the best you can do is to adequately prepare yourself. Interviews are not a perfect form of assessment, and by recognising this, you should accept them as a learning opportunity.

Most interviewers have their favourite questions that may or may not have any apparent bearing on the job for which you have applied. Some of these will have been copied from other people with whom they have been interviewing. Others will be questions asked of them at some point in their career. There's nothing you can do to predict these questions, but try to keep a cool head and do your best to answer them – however strange or irrelevant you might think they are.

Most interviewers set out to take control of the interview and they will do this in a number of different ways. They might begin by setting the scene and telling you the role they wish you to play:

> *'I will begin by asking questions about you and your background and experience and I will then give you some information about the company, the job and pay and benefits. Finally, I shall be pleased to answer any of your questions.'*

Other interviewers are keen to work to a strict checklist approach and will consequently prompt you to move on to the next subject by using statements such as 'Can we now move on to . . .', and will frequently keep an eye on the watch for timing purposes.

The most experienced interviewers control the interview using different questioning techniques and their body language. They are aware that the *way* they ask questions will influence your responses.

Here are some examples of these questioning techniques which vary in degree of structure, but commonly occur in interviews.

## Closed Questions

These questions are framed in such a way to extract only a 'Yes' or 'No' response, for example:

*'Have you always enjoyed selling stationery?'* or;

*'I notice you improved the level of staff morale in your last company'.*

Closed questions are often asked by untrained interviewers and you will be doing yourself no good if you fall into the trap of simply answering with a 'Yes' or 'No'. Remember all your preparation? Well, here is an opportunity to sell yourself and to make use of it. Always elaborate your answers by using illustrations, for example in response to the second question above you might say:

*'Yes, and this brought about a change of response and attitude towards existing customers, whilst at the same time increasing the level of new business.'*

## Open-ended Questions

This approach is intended to get you talking without setting the direction too clearly through the question. The interviewer will find this a useful way to get you to expand on a range of topics, for example:

> 'Tell me about yourself.'
>
> 'What's the difference between management and leadership?'

With this type of question you need to choose your words carefully. Don't be tempted to ramble on or you will often dig a very big hole for yourself. Keep in mind that problems often come with secondary questions: 'Well, that's all well and good, but what about . . .'

## Hypothetical Questions

These are 'What if . . .' questions designed to see how you will respond:

> 'What action would you take if one of your staff insulted a customer?'
>
> 'What would you do if you identified urgent training needs for your staff, but could not release them without levels of work suffering?'

These questions are often put to test your ability to think on your feet. If you are unsure of what the interviewer is driving at, then ask for clarification.

## Probing Questions

Probing questions are aimed at either eliciting more information, getting you to justify what you may have just said, or clarifying a point. However most will be follow-up questions arising from your last response.

> *'How did you solve that particular problem?'*

> *'What did your manager say when you took that course of action?'*

> *'How did the company benefit from your achievements?'*

## Forced Choice Questions

Forced choice questions offer you a choice of two answers that you will be expected to justify, for example:

> *'If you had a choice of including your staff on a leadership training course with staff from this company or in a mix with staff from other companies, which would you choose and why?'*

It is not always easy to understand why such questions are asked – perhaps the interviewer has personally experienced the problem. The best way of dealing with this sort of question is to include a conditioner:

> *'Assuming the course content adequately deals with the sort of issues faced by this company, I would choose a course with a mix of staff from this and other companies. Including staff from companies with different cultures is very often beneficial because they can share their experiences.'*

*Winning at Interviews*

## Technical Questions

These types of questions focus on your work experience and are a test of your technical knowledge:

> *'What do you understand by . . . ?'*
>
> *'Describe some of the recent developments in the industry.'*
>
> *'Give me several examples of . . . ?'*

## Multiple Questions

By their very nature these are confusing questions since the interviewer is really asking several different questions in one:

> *'Tell me what you enjoy most about your current job and if you get the opportunity to spend time out of the office, how often is this and do you find this aspect of your work rewarding?'*

Be sure to respond to these questions in the order they were delivered.

## Summarising Questions

Interviewers use this technique to confirm what you have said:

> *'I assume you mean . . .'*
>
> *'Let me just make sure I understand what you're saying . . .'*

Whichever interviewing technique is used, if you don't

understand a question ask for it to be repeated or reflect it back to make sure your understanding is correct.

There is no point in listing the many hundreds of questions which employers might ask at selection interviews, but I have listed those questions most commonly asked. You may care to study these questions to determine which ones you could be asked at your interview. Bear in mind what you know about the company and the job, and the information you have provided to the employer in your CV, covering letter and application form.

## Interview Questions Most Commonly Asked

1. Tell me about yourself.
2. How would you describe yourself?
3. Why are you applying for this job?
4. What interests you most about this job?
5. What is/was the most difficult and demanding part of your current/last job?
6. What changes were you able to make?
7. What financial responsibilities did you have?
8. What difficulties did you have in dealing with poor performers?
9. If you had your time all over again what changes would you make?
10. What mistakes have you made and what have you learned from them?
11. What are your major strengths?
12. What have been your major achievements?
13. What has been your greatest achievement in any job?
14. What has been the most challenging thing you have ever done?

*Winning at Interviews*

15. What are your greatest weaknesses?
16. What mistakes have you made in the last five years?
17. What can you contribute to this job?
18. How long do you think it will be before you are making an effective contribution in this job?
19. Where do you want to be in three years' time?
20. What are your goals in life?
21. Why should we offer you this job?
22. Why did you leave your last job?
23. Why is there a gap in your work record?
24. Why have you been unemployed for so long?
25. You seem to have had a lot of job moves – why?
26. What is your style of leadership?
27. How do you motivate people?
28. Tell me about the most difficult person you have had to deal with.
29. Have you any positions of responsibility outside of work?
30. Tell me about your leisure interests.
31. In what ways might your current interests be of use in doing this job?
32. What would you do about relocating if you were offered this job?
33. What type of things get you annoyed and frustrated?
34. What sort of training would you need to do this job well?
35. We have a non-smoking policy, how will this affect you?
36. Can you work under pressure?
37. Have you done the best work you are capable of doing?
38. In what way has your job prepared you to take on greater responsibility?
39. Tell me about an event that really challenged you.
40. What are some of the problems you encounter in your job?
41. What are the reasons for your success in this job?

42. What are you outstanding qualities?
43. What do you dislike about your current job?
44. What kind of people do you find it difficult to work with and why?
45. Tell me about your leadership skills.
46. If we offered you this job, how soon would you expect a promotion?
47. Why did you leave your current/last job?
48. Why have you changed jobs so frequently?
49. How many other jobs have you applied for?
50. What are your plans for your own personal development?

## Some Crucial Questions

These are some of the questions which will be asked in one form or another by almost every good interviewer.

### 'Tell me about yourself.'

It is vitally important that your first words impress the interviewer favourably. In a concise two-minute reply tell the interviewer about your education and work experience leading to why you're applying for the job. Try to include something that really helps to sell you.

### 'Why are you looking for another job?'

Always come straight to the point, maintain eye contact and don't take longer than a minute. Why? Because if you take longer, the interviewer will think you're waffling on and this may create suspicion in his mind. If you were made redundant, say so, because being made redundant today doesn't carry the stigma it used to.

*'What are your strengths?'*
High energy level? Enthusiasm? Assertiveness? Decisiveness? Maturity? Social sensitivity? Results? Tough-mindedness? Whatever your strengths, back them up with concrete examples.

*'What are your weaknesses?'*
Don't say 'I can't think of any' – this is sure to work against you since we are all capable of making mistakes. The safest ground is the weakness that is really overuse of a strength. For example: 'Sometimes people mistake my decisiveness for impatience, but I have learned to watch my words.'

*'What have been your most significant achievements?'*
Your earlier efforts spent identifying your achievements should be rewarded at this point, provided you try and match your achievements to the employer's requirements.

*'What can you contribute to this job and the company?'*
The interviewer is trying to establish if you have researched his company. You should be able to handle this question with confidence since you will have obtained copies of the company annual report, staff magazine and spent time in the library collecting useful information.

## Questions which you should ask

This is your last opportunity to create a good impression. Before you launch into a raft of questions, reflect on the information you have already received about the company and the job. Don't ask questions just for the sake of doing so, ask yourself if you really need the information at this stage, be positive and make each and every question count. Here are some examples of questions you might choose from:

- Will there be a further interview?
- Where is the job located?
- What would be your first assignment?
- How often do performance appraisals take place?
- What are the skills and qualities most needed for progression within the company?
- What type of training will be provided?
- Who are the organisation's major competitors?
- How many people work in this department?

Don't discuss salary or benefits. Whilst this information is important, the timing is just wrong. It's far better to wait until you have an offer and to negotiate from that standpoint. It's perfectly acceptable to ask when you might know the outcome of your interview, but don't press for an early decision, this will only annoy the interviewer. Never ask for an assessment of your interview. This is guaranteed to make the interviewer feel awkward and will not help your application.

Finally, maintain your self-confidence right through to the end. Smile, shake hands with the interviewer and offer your thanks for the meeting.

## Controlling interview nerves

Most people will be anxious about attending an interview. Not surprisingly, we all get nerves from time to time, so don't think you've cornered the market. However for some people the prospect of attending a job interview is accompanied by spells of nerves, tension and anxiety that are difficult to control.

Everyone needs to feel anxious at times, it's a perfectly normal state of mind. It causes a reaction that pumps the hormone stimulant adrenaline into the system, spurs people to do challenging things and actually prepares you to cope with difficult situations such as a job interview. What is not desirable is for anxiety to become a problem – for normal temporary feelings of uncertainty, worry or fear to run out of control and interfere with your way of life and what you want to achieve.

Normal anxiety almost always has a cause of which you are aware – for example, an important job interview or a driving test. The good news is that most people are able to manage these feelings. In fact, harnessing the effects of adrenaline often leads to a clarity of mind and thought just when you need it most. So if this is what you experience when attending an interview, just keep telling yourself it's perfectly normal. Of course you'll be eager to present your skills and experience in the best possible light. You'll want to succeed and there's nothing wrong with this kind of anxiety – it's positive.

For people making a career change, anxiety is only a problem when worry or apprehension are experienced frequently, or to a much higher degree than the situation warrants. We can all remember feelings of butterflies in our stomach, dry mouth or sweating before an important event – again, this is perfectly normal. However when anxiety *is* a problem, the rush of adrenaline I mentioned earlier will trigger off certain physiological changes in your body that are difficult to control. These symptoms may include nausea and vomiting, attacks of diarrhoea, insomnia, frequent urinating, panic or palpitations and headaches.

If you are concerned about your anxiety, perhaps because you have suffered recurrent attacks over a period of years, or the symptoms are getting progressively worse in either frequency or severity then you must consult your doctor as soon as possible. In this chapter our aim is to help those people who find that nerves or anxiety are hindering their chances of successful job-search.

There are two important stages in the process of mastering anxiety:

## Stage One

When you experience nerves or anxiety before an interview, it is often because you are worried about failing or not being able to answer a particular question, or that you'll forget something important. In other words you tend to be concerned with damage limitation rather than creating opportunities for success.

Getting yourself back on the straight and narrow means making full use of the advice already given in Chapter 2: The Importance of Positive Thinking. There's no point in worrying about things that might not happen because experience shows that our worst fears seldom do happen. But what if they do? What if you get an interview question you can't answer? Are you going to be negative and say to yourself 'this is just what I expected to happen'? The solution lies in your grasp if you meet the problem head-on. Work out a plan of action and prepare yourself – you'll find all the help you could possibly need included in this chapter and throughout the rest of the book.

There are some messages that are well worth repeating. Having confidence in yourself is one of these. Do you believe in yourself? Are you able to handle situations confidently? If you have answered 'no' to these questions then whatever your feelings about yourself may be, they will be radiated outwards as a silent message others will pick up and respond to.

Imagine for one moment that you overslept this morning and you're feeling off-colour and irritable. You had very little time for breakfast and were 10 minutes late for an important meeting. At this stage you've probably decided that this is going to be a bad day, which invariably it turns out to be. Why? Because you set the scene and the agenda for the day, and it has consequently become what is known as a self-fulfilling prophecy. The silent message you sent out was 'I'm in a bad mood', so everyone either treats you with caution or responds to your negative signals in other ways.

Of course if you have experienced feelings of self-doubt and a lack of confidence for some time, then it's not easy to project positive messages. However, it can be done. Think of the unconscious part of your mind as the hard disk on a computer. It stores many different programs. If these programs happen to be negative, they can be replaced with the positive programs, without the unconscious questioning the change. Just like the computer, your unconscious responds to whatever instructions are received. Here is an example: If you constantly tell yourself that nerves will let you down before or during an interview, the unconscious part of your mind obligingly ensures that this is what will happen. Equally, in reverse, if the message you send to the unconscious part of your mind is that you are confident and sure of yourself, you'll be well on your way to successful interviews and the achievement of a job offer.

Looking your best will also increase your self-confidence; it will help you to believe in yourself and will make others readier to accept your silent positive messages. More about appearance can be found later in this chapter.

To conquer this part of your nerves, the message is simply 'have confidence in yourself and think positive thoughts'.

## Stage Two

In this stage we are dealing with ways to manage the physical symptoms, such as dry mouth, hand shaking and feelings of panic associated with being anxious or nervous.

The first step is to list the symptoms and how they affect you. Bringing things out in the open in this way is part of the healing process.

The best approach is to nip things in the bud and learn to relax. Here are some techniques you can apply almost anytime, anywhere.

**Smile to cheer yourself up**

Try to think of something funny – yes, I'm quite serious! Start with a gentle smile, then slowly broaden it into a big, glowing grin. Many of us already apply this principle without realising. We urge a tearful child to 'Smile', and unwillingly the child smiles – and is cheered up. The point is not to be half-hearted about it – use all the muscles of your face and your eyes to convey the smile.

**Relaxation**

Relaxation can reduce physical symptoms quite dramatically. A well-tried and tested body relaxation technique involves sitting in an upright chair with the small of your back pressed well into the chair. Close your eyes. Sit with your feet flat on the floor and your knees comfortably apart. Place your hands apart in your lap. Take a slow deep breath in. Whilst counting to five, expand your abdomen and tense a group of muscles such as those in the head, forehead, jaw, eyes and face. Slowly exhale counting to five and then gently let go and imagine that the same group of muscles are becoming warm and relaxed. Now do the same with the muscles in your throat, neck and shoulders. Continue with your hands and fingers, up each arm. Now work on your back, abdomen, pelvis, buttocks, legs and feet and finally your toes. Take one last deep breath, exhale and stretch your hands and feet. You can apply this technique anywhere, even whilst sitting in the waiting room before your interview.

You must practice these exercises as often as possible, ideally at different times of the day. In this way you can build up your level of skill in achieving the required level of relaxation. Using this technique to change the way we feel can be a useful tool in helping us through difficult times. As part of a regular routine, it can bring about a marked improvement and eliminate or reduce anxiety.

## Appearance

It is important to recognise that first impressions within an interview count for a great deal. What you wear on the day contributes towards your success or failure. Taking care with your appearance for an interview is not a trivial matter. What you wear is a statement about you and is therefore part of the way you can communicate with others.

Most employers are uncomfortable with extremes that tend to send out the wrong signals. For example, as much as you may prefer to wear casual clothes, they are really a statement of your personality away from work. Very brightly coloured clothes are also almost always unsuitable for everyday work wear. Try to wear something that is fairly formal and conservative but in which you feel comfortable. Try wearing these clothes before the interview – there's nothing worse than finding out that your jacket has a gravy stain on the day of the interview!

Even if you are applying for a job that requires casual clothes, don't be tempted to wear casual clothes for your interview. Your appearance and what you wear is a statement that you value the job for which you have applied and tells the employer something about your attitude to work.

If you are shortlisted for a second interview, I would recommend that you ring the changes and wear something different – if you can afford it. For economy, men could wear a different shirt and tie and women a change of blouse or skirt. The important point is to avoid creating the impression that you have a 'special' interview outfit.

Finally, don't enter the interview room with an array of bags or parcels. These only serve to detract from the favourable impression you wish to create. If you have to bring these items with you, then leave them with the receptionist or security officer.

## Body Language

We all know that first impressions count and nowhere is this more true than when you present yourself for interview. Provided you have done plenty of preparation beforehand, you should feel confident and that confidence should shine through in the way you conduct yourself during the interview. Remember, the interviewer is hoping that the perfect candidate is going to come walking through the door. Enter the room knowing and looking as though you are that perfect candidate.

Body language accounts for about 70 per cent of what we communicate, with tone of voice and the actual words we use accounting for the other 30 per cent. Although the precise percentages vary, the ratios are hardly surprising when you consider that all information reaching our brains can only enter via the five sense – sight, hearing, touch, taste and smell.

Of these senses the eyes are the most valuable, transmitting approximately 85 per cent of the information that reaches our brains. About 10 per cent goes in through our ears and the other senses handle the remaining 5 per cent.

The fact that most of our communication is received visually is in itself no bad thing. The problem is that we put most of our effort into organising and delivering the words we use. Our body language is left to 'fend for itself' and, as a result, tends to come out 'unedited', communicating what we really feel. Where body language is synchronised with what we are saying it supports our spoken communication. Where it is not synchronised it may even contradict our spoken communication, with the result that it will take precedence over the words we have used because people more readily believe what they see rather than what they hear.

So, if the major part of our communication is with body language it makes sense to understand it better, to learn how to use it to support what you want to communicate and to positively influence other people.

## *General Posture*

Your posture is very important, so keep yourself upright. Avoid stooped shoulders and rounded back as these can suggest a lack of confidence. When seated good posture is essential, so don't slump in the chair as if you were at home watching the TV. This is far too over-relaxed a position, and suggests that you may not be taking the interview seriously enough.

## Shaking hands

Do not be the first to offer a handshake, but be quick to respond when the interviewer offers their hand in greeting. It is possible to tell quite a lot from your handshake, so don't shake hands as if you are intending to crush fingers or grind knuckles, and don't use your other hand to grasp the interviewer's wrist, upper arm or shoulder. This is too domineering and will make the interviewer feel uncomfortable. Equally, don't give a sweaty and limp handshake reminiscent of a 'pound of wet fish' as this gives the opposite signal of being submissive. Finally, don't hold the interviewer's hand for too long, as this signals over-familiarity.

So, if body language is so important, what is the best way to conduct yourself during the interview? Here are some tips for keeping track of those negative mannerisms and gestures:

## Hand and arm gestures

Most people attending interviews have a problem knowing what to do with their arms and hands. Here are the main areas of concern:

- Avoid crossing your arms in front of you or holding hands with yourself. This is a closed body or closed attitude position that will only serve to make you and the interviewer feel uncomfortable.
- Don't fidget with rings, watch, cufflinks, handbags or purses etc. To the trained observer these gestures are a dead giveaway that you are attempting to conceal your nervousness.
- Keep your hands away from your face. For example, don't cover your mouth with your hand, touch your nose, rub your eye or pull your collar – it can suggest you are not being entirely honest.

- Don't rub your ear – this can mean you're trying to block out the interviewer's words.
- Don't scratch your neck – this can signal doubt or uncertainty.
- Don't put your fingers in your mouth as this signals that you are under pressure and need reassurance.
- Don't put your hands behind your head – it is a gesture used by the *know-it-all* and other people can often find this irritating.

**Aim at a neutral position for your hands. Keep them resting on your knees, but don't be tempted to clench your hands together.**

## Leg gestures

Crossed legs are often seen, like crossed arms, as a negative or defensive gesture. Follow the advice given previously to avoid crossing your arms in front of you. Adopt a comfortable position, keeping your legs together and both feet on the ground, without locking your ankles.

## Face

We have little control over our facial muscles, so as a result our face is the most expressive part of our bodies.

The area around the eyes and mouth are the most expressive. Raised eyebrows and a 'O'-shaped open mouth signifies surprise but raised eyebrows and an open smile indicates real pleasure; knotted eyebrows and a downturned mouth signify sadness while knotted eyebrows and tightly pursed lips signify displeasure. There is hardly a single emotion that does not show in the face in such a way as to be instantly recognisable by someone else.

## Eyes

Although the eyes are part of the face they are important enough to warrant specific mention. The effect of the eyes can be extremely subtle – for example we tend to feel uneasy about people with 'beady little eyes' (small pupils).

Eye contact is important in an interview. If you avoid eye contact with the interviewer you may appear lacking in confidence or disinterested. If your eye contact is too intense, you may appear aggressive and make the interviewer feel uncomfortable. But if your eye contact is immediate and moderate (about 50-70 per cent of the time) you will give an entirely different impression, especially if accompanied by a pleasant facial expression. In effect you are saying 'I am pleased to meet you, I feel confident in myself, I am looking forward to the interview'.

## Tone of Voice

Tone of voice is an important aspect of our communication. If it is too quiet and hesitant the interviewer will think you are nervous. If it is too loud, too fast and abrupt, the interviewer will think you are impatient. Throughout the interview you should pay attention to:

- **volume** – so that you can be heard;
- **pace** – so that you sound enthusiastic and relaxed; and
- **pitch** – a low, slow monotone can make you sound bored; a high, rapid voice delivered in fits and starts can make you sound nervous. Pitch therefore needs to be moderate and varied.

## Interviews make us nervous

Of course interviews can make us nervous, and as a consequence we tend to resort to irritating gestures more frequently. If you are not sure whether you do use these gestures, then ask your partner or a close friend to tell you. Once you are aware, you can work at stopping them yourself.

## Be Positive!

To use body language to your advantage in the interview, you must ensure that it is positive. I have grouped some aspects of body language together into positive and negative to illustrate this point. The negative has been further sub-divided into submissive/inferior and aggressive/superior. No prizes for guessing which is which!

### Positive

Smile
Interested expression
Moderate eye contact
Sufficient volume, varied pace and pitch of voice
Open posture
Hands and arms support what is being said

### Negative

| | |
|---|---|
| Wobbly voice | Hard voice |
| Slow speech | Rapid speech |
| Worried expression | Extremes of expression |
| Evasive looks downward | Excessive eye contact |
| Mouth covered with hand | Finger wagging/jabbing |

# On the Day of the Interview

Here is a list of dos and don'ts for the day of the interview:

## Do's

**Do** make sure you know how to get to the interview destination. If you have any doubts ask the employer to send you a map of the local area and plan your journey in good time.

**Do** get yourself ready in good time. Be neatly groomed and conservatively dressed and you'll feel much more comfortable if you stick to wearing something you've worn before.

**Do** arrive at your destination with ten minutes to spare. Being late for the interview is the eighth deadly sin. When you arrive, be courteous with everyone you meet, starting with receptionists and secretaries. Remember they may be asked for an opinion of the applicants by some interviewers.

**Do** be observant. Take a good look around and try to form an impression of the company.

**Do** start positively by making eye contact with the interviewer, shake hands firmly and wait to be invited to sit down.

**Do** be careful about your body language because it is very revealing and many interviewers take an interest in how you express yourself through your non-verbal behaviour. Interviewers will start to make observations as soon as you enter the room and they will react differently towards you, depending on their interpretation of your initial impact. Friendly eye contact is important, but don't overdo it, maintain only enough to keep their attention, since you might make the interviewer feel ill at ease. Smile in a friendly manner. Don't slouch. Sit well back in the chair, keep your hands on your lap unless you want to use them to express yourself and don't shuffle your feet or change the position of your legs too often.

**Do** maintain a positive attitude throughout the interview. This is by far the best way to control your nerves. Try to really work at it. The biggest fear is probably the fear of making a fool of yourself, but does it really matter? Ask yourself what is the worst that can happen and get the interview into perspective. If you've done all your preparation, you can constantly reassure yourself that you have nothing to worry about. Think positively about yourself, your skills and abilities and you have no reason to be nervous.

**Do** listen carefully throughout the interview and always let the speaker talk without interruption.

**Do** avoid tea/coffee and biscuits. They are almost impossible to deal with in an interview.

**Do** maintain a positive approach throughout the interview. When the interview is finished, close with a firm handshake.

**Do** make use of all the research and information you gathered before the interview. Stress all the key aspects of your background, experience, transferable skills and achievements that are a match for the employer's requirements. Find opportunities to introduce the information you obtained about the company.

## *Don'ts*
**Don't** smoke.

**Don't** chew gum.

**Don't** be over-familiar with the interviewer. Never use Christian names, no matter how informally you are addressed. Take things seriously but try to demonstrate a sense of humour.

**Don't** take notes.

**Don't** offer references or proof of qualifications during the interview unless you are asked to do so.

**Don't** lean or rest on the interviewer's desk.

**Don't** be modest – sell yourself instead.

**Don't** correct the interviewer.

**Don't** raise matters of salary, particularly during a first interview – unless you are specifically asked about them.

## *Reviewing your Performance*

Take the opportunity to review your interview performance, as soon as you can – whilst the event is still fresh in your mind. Record the names and titles of those you met at the interview, as much about the job as possible and what they regard as the key tasks. Ask yourself what aspects of the interview were good and which were poor. Why do you think these aspects were poor? This is particularly important if you are not offered the job, because you will need to improve on these aspects for future interviews.

# 14

# Other Selection Methods

*'If you have knowledge, let others light their candles by it'*
Margaret Fuller

Apart from the interview, what other selection methods do companies use in the pursuit of the perfect applicant?

Just as an applicant can experience different standards with the selection interview, companies can sometimes use other selection methods that are inappropriate and unprofessionally managed. However most companies appreciate the value of using valid selection methods, backed by empirical evidence, which show who is going to be the most effective applicant.

Selection methods can range from the most straightforward to the bizarre. Here are just a few of those you might encounter.

## Selection Tests

### A brief history

It may surprise you to read that tests have been around for quite a long time. In fact, it was at the turn of the century that a number of tests were developed for educational selection and in the diagnosis of mental retardation in children.

At the outbreak of the Second World War, millions of men

and women were called to arms. By then, testing had become sufficiently sophisticated to enable individuals to be screened for different service occupations. After the war, tests gradually found their way into everyday employment practice and were developed and adapted for the needs of industry and commerce.

During the 1970s, strong views were expressed by those in favour and those opposed to tests. Indeed, testing was seen as running contrary to the spirit of fair employment practice and the progressive liberal attitudes of the 1970s so at that time acquired a bad name. As a result of this bad publicity for tests, psychologists set about collecting data that enabled them to devise tests that were more job related but less biased.

Since the mid 1980s, selection tests have become much more popular in the UK, and their usage has boomed. This is due to the fact that fairer and better researched tests have been developed and because employers have been trained in the administration and interpretation of test results. The signs are that in the changing climate of British industry, selection tests are here to stay.

## What are selection tests?

Selection tests are, as the name suggests, tests that are designed and used for the purpose of selecting people for jobs, promotion or transfer. They are also used in redundancy and career counselling.

In selection, the purpose of a test is to provide an objective means of measuring individual abilities and characteristics. Usually such tests have standardised sets of questions or problems that allow an applicant's results to be compared with those of other people of a similar background. For example, if you happen to be a manager, your test results would be

## Other Selection Methods

compared with those of a large and representative group of other managers who are known as the 'norm' sample.

Employers have come to recognise that the right tests are at least as effective and more often so than most other selection methods. However the greatest growth has come in the use of personality measures that fall within the definition of tests but are more commonly called inventories or questionnaires to emphasise the fact that there are no right or wrong answers.

Today, employers are equally concerned about whether the applicant will 'fit in'. 'Has done is the best guide to will do' was the watchword of the 1960s and 1970s. Now, employers are concerned that 'Has done it this way' means 'Won't want to do it any other way'. Today there is a heightened recognition of the impact of personal makeup on many jobs and a new emphasis on the need to take account of personality in building and maintaining effective teams.

Provided that tests are valid and reliable, employers can use them to help improve the selection process and to lessen subjectivity. Many companies also find tests a more cost-effective way of dealing with a large response to recruitment advertising.

## The variety of selection tests

In this section, we shall take a look at the many different types of selection tests that are used by employers as part of their selection process.

### Tests of ability

Assessment of ability is perhaps the most commonly used test in the field of employment. Ability tests tend to fall into two groups: aptitude tests and attainment tests. Aptitude tests are used to predict the potential of a candidate for a particular job.

Here are some of the ability tests you could encounter in the form of paper and pencil tests and practical exercises:

**Verbal Reasoning**
These are about how well you understand ideas expressed in words and how you think and reason with words.

**Numerical Reasoning**
These tests are geared to identify your understanding and reasoning with numbers.

**Clerical Skills**
These tests usually deal with checking and classifying data, quickly and accurately.

**Diagrammatic Reasoning and Mechanical Reasoning**
As their names suggest, these tests deal with diagrams and mechanical concepts.

**Abstract Reasoning**
These tests set out to identify how good you are at thinking in abstract terms.

There are also aptitude tests that measure spatial abilities and motor ability (manual dexterity).

A significant development in the last decade has been the production of attainment tests that measure abilities or skills already acquired by training or experience, for example typing or PC skills. If you are asked to take an attainment test as part of a selection process this can often say more to the prospective employer about your skills than comparing candidates' qualifications.

## Other Selection Methods

### General intelligence tests

The difficulty with intelligence tests is that they are based on a person's IQ or intelligence quotient. Intelligence is a highly complex concept and psychologists cannot agree on a definition. Because of the variety of definitions, there are a similar variety of tests. The most popular among recruiters are those which have been properly validated, where test scores can be compared with *norms* in such a way as to indicate how those taking the test compare with the rest of the population. Such tests often include a variety of questions such as similarities, opposites, numeracy, vocabulary and more general subjects.

### Personality tests

This next area of testing is the assessment of personality or behaviour. Again there are many different theories of personality and consequently, many different types of personality tests.

One definition of personality is 'the relatively stable and enduring aspects of individuals that distinguish them from other people'. These aspects are sometimes described as personality traits, and are the basis of the belief that people are predisposed to behave in certain ways in a variety of different situations. The assumption that people are consistent in the ways they express these traits are the basis for making predictions about their future behaviour.

The main characteristics that personality tests aim to identify in an applicant are:

| | |
|---|---|
| Extroversion | Introversion |
| Tough minded | Tender minded |
| Independent | Dependent |
| High self-confidence | Low self-confidence |

Examples of personality tests in common use include self-report questionnaires. These are based on the measurement of traits such as who is the most assertive, trusting, competitive, or conscientious etc. The usual format is a questionnaire where applicants are required to identify which of a number of responses best, or sometimes least well, describes their view of themselves or their reactions to a given situation. Perhaps the most well-known classification of traits is that produced by Cattell. It forms the basis for the Sixteen Personality Factor Questionnaire more commonly known as the 16PF personality test. Similar tests include the Myers-Briggs Type Indicator, the Saville and Holdsworth Occupational Questionnaire (OPQ) and the Gordon Personal Profile and Inventory.

*Interest questionnaires* are sometimes used to supplement personality tests. They assess the preferences of respondents for particular types of occupation and are therefore more applicable to vocational guidance.

*Value questionnaires* attempt to assess beliefs about what is desirable or good or what is undesirable or bad. The questionnaires measure the relative prominence of such values as conformity, independence, achievement, decisiveness and orderliness.

Applicants may often be faced with a battery of tests that include tests of intelligence, aptitude and personality. More employers are finding it important to feed back the results of personality tests to applicants, since it enables the recruiter and the applicant to discuss more fully the whole issue of the applicant's character. If this benefit is not offered to you by the recruiter then do ask if feedback can be provided.

## What to expect if you are asked to sit a test

Most tests are conducted under 'examination' type conditions.

## Other Selection Methods

This is to ensure that all candidates are treated exactly the same.

The test may take place immediately prior to an interview, but will quite often be held separately to give time to check the test results. When you arrive at the test venue you will be greeted by the test administrator, who will provide you with all the materials you will need, such as test booklets, answer sheets and pencils.

The administrator will explain the test procedure. This often includes a strict time limit for the test, with the exception of personality tests, which you will be asked to complete as quickly as possible.

Most tests have a few example questions for you to complete before starting the test proper. This is a good idea since it helps you to understand the nature of the test. Quite often the administrator will give you an opportunity to ask questions. If you are unsure about any aspect of the test you must speak up at this stage since you won't have the opportunity again.

Once the test is over, the administrator will gather together the test booklets and answer papers. These will be given to a person in the company qualified to mark and interpret the test results. Each candidate's test results are called a raw score. On its own, a raw score means nothing, since it has to be compared with that of a similar group of people. Taking the earlier example of a manager, your test results would then be compared with those of other managers and may be either average, above average or below average compared to the rest of that group.

## Preparing a test strategy can help

A few simple rules can help when faced with a selection test. Getting a good night's sleep before the test is essential. Also, you need to be alert so don't drink alcohol before a test. Try to keep calm and face the world with confidence.

Test administrators will advise you not to spend too much time on particular questions. This is really good advice, especially if you are taking a personality test. If you are taking an ability test and the answer to a question eludes you, move on to the next one. If there is time then go back to the question you have missed.

Follow the test instructions precisely. Always make sure that you are placing your answers in the correct place on the answer sheet and if you're asked to circle one answer from a choice of four, then don't make the mistake of putting a cross through the answer.

## Assessment Centres

An assessment centre is a programme (not a place!) which lasts from one to three days and uses a range of assessment techniques to determine whether or not applicants are suitable for a particular job. Assessment centres can also be used for promotion purposes and diagnosing development needs.

The usual format of an assessment centre are interviews, psychometric tests and one or two days of role-playing exercises with the focus on behaviour. The role-playing exercises are used to capture and simulate the key dimensions of the job, assuming that individual performance in these exercises predicts behaviour on the job. These exercises include one-to-one and group role-plays and sometimes also include interviews and written exercises.

During the role-playing exercises, participants' performance is measured by trained assessors. Meal times are often seen as a continuation of the assessment process so you should always be on your guard.

As with the selection tests, don't be afraid to ask the selecting organisation for feedback from your attendance at the assessment centre.

## Job Simulations

This is a selection technique that attempts to take a small piece of the type of work that the candidate will be expected to do in the job in question, and perform it under observation at the time of selection. There are several different ways of applying this technique but they are usually written or oral exercises. Those of the written variety often expect the candidate to deal with an 'in-tray' of letters, reports, messages and internal memos. In the oral exercise, candidates can be expected to make presentations or take part in group discussions.

## Graphology

Graphology is the study of handwriting. The UK has been slow to adopt this technique for selection purposes, compared with 80 per cent of major companies in West Germany and as many as half of the major companies in Switzerland. In the United States more than 3,000 companies now use handwriting analysis for various business reasons.

Graphologists study more than 300 signs in your handwriting – including slant, pressure, spacing, margins, how you form and connect various letters, and how your signature compares with your writing. Each sign must be interpreted in the context of the handwriting as a whole.

Graphologists say that handwriting can reveal hidden talents and traits as well as serious flaws. In some countries graphologists now offer personal career counselling, believing they may be able to discover untapped gifts that could lead to a fulfilling career.

Despite its wide use on the continent of Europe, graphology remains controversial and there is little evidence of its predictive value. The general experience in the UK suggests there is little chance of a strong growth in its use, not least because of the dependence on individual interpretation by specialists whose reputations vary.

PERSONNEL MANAGER: "YOUR EDUCATION IS FIRST-RATE, YOUR EXPERIENCE IN THE BUSINESS IS AWESOME AND YOUR REFERENCES ARE BRILLIANT, BUT WE WERE RATHER HOPING FOR A GEMINI IN THE ASCENDANCY."

# 15

# Coping with Rejection and the Job Offer

*'Of all the sad words of tongue or pen,
the saddest are these: "It might have been".'*
John Greenleaf Whittier

## After the interview

Every interview should be a learning experience, after which you must ask yourself 'how can I improve my performance?'

As soon as possible after attending the interview, write down your impressions of what went well and what went badly. Try and describe your responses to difficult questions and the interviewer's reactions. If you feel your responses were not satisfactory, then spend some time deciding how you would tackle these questions at future interviews. If you feel you could have done better, how could you improve?

## Coping with Rejection

If you receive a letter of rejection after an interview you will naturally feel disappointed. However, as I mentioned in Chapter 2, it is important that you rise above this disappointment, to get on with your life and to continue your job search with a positive attitude. In these cases, learning from your experience is an essential part of the recovery process.

Some books on job-hunting suggest you should write or even telephone asking for feedback. Frankly, I would disagree with this advice. Put yourself in the interviewer's shoes. If everyone who was rejected asked for feedback then a good part of the interviewer's time would be spent on this unproductive activity. Even telling someone that their experience in a particular area is a little weak can often invite a retaliatory response that defends the quantity and quality of their experience. You can't blame the interviewer for taking a dim view of requests for feedback.

Instead of asking for feedback you should consider sending a short letter thanking the interviewer for their time and asking to be considered for any suitable posts which occur in the future.

## The Job Offer

Success at last, you've been offered a job!

The ideal scenario would be to receive several job offers at the same time so that you can consider which is the best for you. Unfortunately this does seem to be very much the exception rather than the rule. If you have only one offer to consider, it is sometimes suggested that you reject the first offer – if you've been out of work for some time you may be desperate enough to take on the wrong job. What is the best way of dealing with this situation?

Clearly you need time to properly consider the offer. It's never discourteous to ask the employer for a date by which they would expect you to reply. This is a way of buying yourself some time in which to carefully consider one of the most important decisions of your life.

The sort of factors you will need to take into account in

## Coping with Rejection and the Job Offer

determining whether the job is right for you will include:

- The company – whether it is an expanding or contracting organisation and the impressions gained from attending for interview
- The nature of the duties and accountabilities (have you seen a copy of the job description?) and to whom you will report
- Opportunities for progression within the company
- Where will you work?
- Salary and methods of review; details of performance related pay and bonus arrangements
- Fringe benefits including company car
- Details of assistance with relocation expenses
- Pension arrangements
- Sickness benefits
- Hours of work
- Period of notice
- The quality of the offer of employment documentation

If you are unsure about any of these factors, then do seek clarification from the employer. If the salary is not quite up to your expectations then you may need to do a little gentle negotiating. If the company has a personnel manager or you were routed to the company via a search and selection specialist then it is best to use these intermediaries. Tell them that you are delighted with the job offer and are anxious to join their company, but the salary is lower than you expected. By this stage they will be anxious to conclude the recruitment exercise and this should work in your favour.

One other reason for buying yourself some time is if you have attended other interviews and are waiting to hear the results. You can put some gentle pressure on the other employers to try and produce decisions within your timeframe.

# 16

# Working For Yourself

*'I find the great thing in this world is not so much where we stand, as in what direction we are moving'*
O. W. Holmes

If you have been thinking about working for yourself, you will be joining an increasing army of people who have already done so.

Many people think the prospect of self-employment must be better than working for someone else, but they may not have the foggiest idea of what is involved in running their business or the kind of business they wish to start.

## Do You Have What it Takes?

Not everyone is cut out for self-employment. Consequently you need to think through very carefully whether you have the right personal qualities in addition to a good idea, the finance and the skills to manage a business.

Amongst the essential qualities are those of the capacity for hard work, a good supply of enthusiasm, dedication and persistence, plenty of self-confidence, planning and organising ability, initiative and problem-solving skills and of course the ability to sell. Finally, running a business can be lonely – can you cope with this?

Before you plunge in with more enthusiasm than thoughtfulness, sit down quietly for a couple of hours and give yourself an honest assessment. Apart from being physically and mentally capable of starting your own business, you need to ask yourself why you are going into business and what you expect to achieve.

The support of your family is absolutely essential if you wish to start your own business. For example, if you're going to work from home, will someone be prepared to answer your phone when you are out? Will someone help you with the paperwork or the accounts? Do they understand the amount of time you will have to devote to the business, particularly in the first few years? Are they willing to accept the financial risks involved? Only if you can answer 'Yes' to all those questions should you be thinking seriously about self-employment.

## Advice and Guidance

Various forms of help and support for those thinking of starting their own business are available and your local library or Jobcentre will have details of what is on offer at your local Chamber of Commerce or the Training and Enterprise Councils (TECs). Enterprise Agencies set up by the TECs provide an advice and counselling service about self-employment together with seminars and training on a variety of subjects including marketing and taxation. There is also a free business helpline which gives details of local training courses.

To overcome the drawback of losing Jobseeker's Allowance, financial support is available during the business start-up period for 26 weeks. To obtain the address of your local Enterprise Agency look for the telephone number of the Training and Enterprise Council in your local telephone directory.

## The Business Plan

If, after taking advantage of all the free advice and guidance you can get, you still believe you could be on the way to making a successful business, then the next step is to organise and plan your business using a business plan. Don't think that your business plan is there just to impress your bank manager; it is an essential blueprint to help you set your goals and recognise your strengths and weaknesses. A detailed business plan is a disciplined way of helping you to forecast your cash requirements for items such as premises, marketing and promotional costs, equipment, systems and administration, salaries for those people you may employ, payments to solicitors and accountants and National Insurance Contributions. It will also enable you to forecast your sales and profit, based on a detailed assessment of the market for your product or service. Once done, it will stop you from dreaming up ideas along the road which, though good in themselves, may be too costly or too early to introduce into your first year of business.

To obtain free advice on preparing your business plan, speak to the Training and Enterprise Councils (see Chapter 17 for details of this and other useful organisations).

## Legal Identities

To set up in business, you will need to have one of the following legal identities:

### Sole Trader

As the name suggests, this is a business owned in its entirety by one person. The person and the business are legally one and the same. If a trading name is used, the legal reality is that it is, for example, 'David Smith trading as DS Motor Repairs'.

It follows that whilst the proprietor is entitled to all the profits from the business, the main disadvantage of being a sole trader is that you are personally liable for all your business debts since all the financial risk is taken by one person. All the assets, business and personal, are included in that financial risk, since there is no method by which personal assets can be separated from the business.

You do not have to submit accounts to Company House, neither are you subject to the laws affecting company directors under the Companies Act. But you will have to pay National Insurance Contributions for yourself and anyone you employ and you will have to submit annual accounts to H M Inspector of Taxes. If you decide to register for VAT you will also need to maintain records for H M Customs and Excise.

## Partnerships

This is a firm where two or more people have a written or verbal agreement to run that business jointly. The same conditions apply as for a sole trader. However when it comes to liability for debts, the law says that all partners are jointly and severally responsible. This means that all the partners (jointly) are and each individual partner (severally) is responsible for all the partners' liabilities. Therefore if a partner has agreed a share of 40 per cent of the business, he is still responsible for 100 per cent of the partnership liabilities, plus if you close the business down and none of your partners can pay the debts of the business, then the creditors can sue you for the full amount owed.

Partnership agreements are vital to protect the interest of all partners. Whilst the law sets out the way liabilities are dealt with, a proper written agreement drawn up between the partners lays down the way in which the partnership should be run. It should deal with such matters as the role of each partner, the apportioning of profits or losses, arrangements for admitting new partners or a partner leaving, the operation of the bank account and the effect of a partner being found guilty of a criminal offence, for example fraud.

Without an agreement, there is no mechanism for removing a partner who behaves in any way contrary to the interests of the partnership. For these reasons I would strongly advise anyone thinking of setting up a partnership to seek the advice of a solicitor in drawing up the agreement.

## Limited Company

In setting up a limited company, you are creating a new legal entity in law. A company can sue and be sued just like a person through the civil courts, and any monies paid come from the company funds and not from the pockets of the directors. A limited company must have at least two shareholders, one director and a company secretary who could be a second director.

The concept behind the company format is that those who put capital into the company become shareholders in proportion to the amount of capital injected. Shareholders are rewarded by receiving dividends in proportion to their shares and are eligible to attend the Annual General Meeting to approve or otherwise the way in which the company has been run by the directors. The meeting will also determine how much of the profit shall be distributed to the shareholders as dividends and how much should be retained in the company for future use.

Control of the company is in the hands of the directors

who are appointed by the shareholders to manage its affairs. In small limited companies, the chances are that the directors are also shareholders.

Directors are responsible for ensuring that their company complies with the law, particularly the Companies Act. They must not continue to trade if the company is insolvent and must act in the best interests of their creditors.

The main advantage of a limited company over a sole trader is the shareholders' limitation of liability for debts. If you want to form a limited company you can do this for yourself, but for around £200 it is safer to put in the hands of a solicitor. You can have a company set up tailor made from scratch, or you can buy one off the shelf and even get the name changed for around £100. In all cases the name of the company must be registered when you file the details with Companies House and must not be too similar to any other existing company. You will also need to obtain a Certificate of Incorporation before you start trading as a limited company.

Professional tax and accounting advice is almost essential for a limited company and an annual professional audit is a statutory requirement. You must also submit a copy of your annual accounts to Companies House where these details are open to public examination.

## Franchising

There are a growing number of people running their own businesses – ranging from plumbing and dry-cleaning to timber preservation and restaurants – through the system of franchise. As franchisees, or licence-holders, they buy the exclusive right to market, in an agreed territory, products or services already established by a major company.

Hundreds of companies now sell franchises in this country with an annual turnover in excess of £11 billion. Because advertising, training, supply and other services are provided by the franchisor, a franchise can have a much better chance of succeeding than an independent company.

To begin with you need to find a business that you will enjoy and can afford. There are opportunities at all price levels from around £4000 to others priced as high as £300,000. You can find out what is on offer in the quarterly magazine *Franchise World*. On top of finding the initial outlay you will also need sufficient funds to cover the day-to-day running costs of the franchise. In exchange for the support, guidance and use of names and trade marks, the franchisor usually expects a percentage of gross sales.

Buying a franchise can be confusing so you would be well advised to seek professional advice from the British Franchise Association which monitors the professional standards of its members and studies all aspects of franchising. Also consult your bank manager, solicitor and accountant. The British Franchise Association can supply you with a list of those advisors who have a thorough knowledge of franchising.

Don't be tempted to part with your money until you have established that the promoting company is experienced and successful, and that there is a demand for its products or services. Don't be tempted by a glossy brochure or videotape. Do a company search – the Companies Registration Office has details on directors, financial status, staff and history. Request a bank reference and get your accountant to scrutinise the company's balance sheet. Finally, armed with a list of questions, arrange a meeting with the franchise senior management and insist on meeting existing franchisees, preferably ones who have been operating for years.

*Manage Your Career*

A useful franchise information pack can be obtained from the British Franchise Association whose address and telephone number can be found in Chapter 17 – Useful Souces of Information.

SECRETARY: "I HEARD YOU LEFT THE COMPANY TO BECOME SELF EMPLOYED. HOW'S IT GOING?"

FRIEND: "TO TELL THE TRUTH, I NEVER KNEW HOW STUPID BOSSES COULD BE UNTIL I STARTED WORKING FOR MYSELF."

# 17
# Useful Sources of Information

## Contents

Careers
Job search
National Newspaper Advertisements
Interim Management
Self Employment
The Voluntary Sector
Further Education
Employment Advice
Pensions, Investments and Financial Planning
Benefits and Entitlements
Taxation
Health

## Careers

### Publications
*The A-Z of Careers and Jobs*, Diane Burston (Kogan Page).
*Britain's Best Employers? A Job Hunter's Guide*, Sean Hamil (Kogan Page).
*British Vocational Qualifications* (Kogan Page).
*Careers Encyclopaedia*, Audrey Segal & Katherine Lea (Cassell).

*The Careers Guide*, Madeleine Bostock & Lindsay Taylor (Cascaid).
*Occupations*, Judy Leavesley (Careers & Occupational Information Centre).
*The Penguin Career Guide*, Anna Alston & Anna Daniel (Penguin).

*Useful Addresses & Telephone Numbers:*
*The Careers Service* – Look in your phone book for your local office.

## Job Search

*Publications*
*CEPEC Recruitment Guide* – CEPEC Publications, Kent House, 41 East Street, Bromley, Kent BR1 1QQ. (Lists some 700 recruitment agencies in the UK).
*The Executive Grapevine* – Similar guide to CEPEC and is available from Executive Grapevine Ltd, 79 Manor Way, Blackheath, London SE3 9XG.
*BRAD – The Monthly Guide to Media Selection*. Helpful in locating regional and local newspapers, trade and professional magazines and journals. Can be found in most libraries.

*Useful Addresses & Telephone Numbers:*
*Jobcentres* – Look in the phone book for your local office.

*Useful Sources of Information*

| **National Newspaper Advertisements** | | |
|---|---|---|
| Newspaper | Days of the Week | Sector |
| Daily Mail | Tuesday | Clerical Secretarial |
| | Thursday | Clerical Engineering General Appointments Overseas Printing and Publishing Retail Sales Technical |
| Daily Telegraph | Thursday | Executive/Management General Appointments |
| The European | Wednesday | General appointments in the European Community |
| The Express | Thursday | Catering/Hotel Engineering General Appointments Sales Technical |
| Financial Times | Wednesday | Banking Finance General Appointments |
| | Thursday | Accountancy Finance |

| Newspaper | Days of the Week | Sector |
|---|---|---|
| Guardian | Monday | Creative and Media |
| | | Fund raising |
| | | Marketing |
| | | PR |
| | | Sales |
| | | Secretarial |
| | Tuesday | Education |
| | | General Appointments |
| | Wednesday | Environment |
| | | Health |
| | | Housing |
| | | Public Sector |
| | Saturday | Careers |
| | | Creative and Media |
| | | Education |
| | | General Appointments |
| | | Graduates |
| | | IT |
| | | Marketing |
| | | PR |
| | | Public Sector |
| | | Sales |
| | | Science |
| Independent | Tuesday | IT |
| | Wednesday | Accounting |
| | | Banking |
| | | Clerical |
| | | Finance |
| | | Legal |

## Useful Sources of Information

| Newspaper | Days of the Week | Sector |
|---|---|---|
| Independent | Wednesday | Office Multilingual Secretarial |
| | Thursday | Education Graduates General Appointments |
| Independent on Sunday | Sunday | All |
| Mail on Sunday | Sunday | All |
| Observer | Sunday | IT |
| Scotsman | Monday | General Appointments |
| | Tuesday | General Appointments |
| | Wednesday | Education General Appointments |
| | Thursday | General Appointments Public Sector |
| | Friday | General Appointments Marketing Sales |
| Sunday Telegraph | Sunday | Direct repeat of Thursday's appointments supplement |
| Sunday Times | Sunday | All |
| The Times | Tuesday | Legal |
| | Wednesday | IT Multilingual |

| Newspaper | Days of the Week | Sector |
|---|---|---|
| The Times | Wednesday | Secretarial |
| | Thursday | Management |
| | | Senior Appointments |
| | | Secretarial |
| | Friday | Education |
| | | Marketing |
| | | Media |
| | | Sales |

## Interim Management

### Publications
*The Personnel Manager's Yearbook*, AP Information Services, Roman House, 296 Golders Green Road, London NW11 9PZ. Telephone 0181 455 4550.

### Useful Addresses & Telephone Numbers
*The Association of Temporary and Interim Executive Services* – 36-38 Mortimer Street, London W1N 7RB. Telephone 0171 323 4300.

## Self Employment

### Publications
*Small Firms Service* – Run by the Department of Employment. Has 13 offices in England, Scotland and Wales. A basic 'Business Start-up Information Pack' covering setting up in business, accounting, marketing and finance etc can be obtained from your local office. Dial 100 and ask the operator for 0800 222999.

## Useful Sources of Information

*The Small Business Guide* – Sources of help in setting up your own business. BBC Publications.

*Starting Your Own Business* – A very useful pamphlet produced by the Inland Revenue, the Contributions Agency and HM Customs & Excise. Available from any of these sources.

## *Useful Addresses & Telephone Numbers:*

*British Franchise Association* – Franchise Chambers, Thames View, Newtown Road, Henley-on-Thames, Oxon RG9 1HG. Telephone 01491 578049.

*Chambers of Commerce* – Look in your phone book or ask at your local library for address and telephone details.

*Companies House* – Notes for guidance and general information can be obtained by contacting the Central Enquiry Unit on 01222 380801.

*Federation of Small Businesses* – Telephone 01235 720911.

*Instant Muscle* – A national charity that helps unemployed people to set up their own business. Their address is Instant Muscle, Springside House, 84 North East Road, London W14 9ES. Telephone 0171 603 2604.

*Institute of Small Businesses* – 14 Willow Street, London EC2A 4BH. Telephone 0171 638 4939.

*The Prince's Scottish Youth Business Trust* – Mercantile Chambers, 53 Bothwell Street, Glasgow G2 6TA.

*The Prince's Youth Business Trust* – 5 Cleveland Place, London SW1Y 6JJ. Telephone 0171 321 6500.

*Training and Enterprise Councils (TECs); Local Enterprise Councils (LECs) in Scotland; Training and Employment Agency in Northern Ireland* – look in your phone book or ask at your Jobcentre or local library for address and telephone details.

# The Voluntary Sector

## Publications
The Voluntary Agencies Directory – Contains a list of nearly 2,000 voluntary organisations and can be obtained from the National Council for Voluntary Organisations, 26 Bedford Square, London WC1V 3HV. Telephone 0171 713 6161

## Useful Addresses & Telephone Numbers
*Charity Recruitment* – This is a recruitment agency for voluntary organisations.
Address: The Garden Studio, 11-15 Betterton Street, London WC2H 9BP. Telephone 0171 833 0770
*REACH* – (Retired Executives Action Clearing House) This is a recruitment agency who maintain a register of retired and redundant people with business or professional expertise wanting to work for out-of-pocket expenses only as part-time volunteers in local charities needing their skills.
Address: REACH, 89 Southwark Street, London SE1 0HD. Telephone 0171 928 0452

# Further Education

## Publications
*British Qualifications* – A useful source of all qualifications in Britain, published by Kogan Page.
*Directory of Further Education*. Comprehensive guide to further education courses in the UK. Published annually by CRAC.
*Independent Careers*. Published by Bloomsbury.
*Stepping Up: A Mature Student's Guide to Higher Education*. A very useful booklet available free from ACAS, Fulton House,

## Useful Sources of Information

Jessop Avenue, Cheltenham, Glos GL50 3SH.
*Students Grants and Loans.* A free booklet published by the DEE. This should be available in Careers/Adult Guidance Centres.

### Useful Addresses & Telephone Numbers:
*The Association of British Correspondence Colleges* – Telephone 0181 544 9559
*MBA Career Guide* – 49 Murray Mews, Camden, London W1 9RH.
*Open University* – Central Enquiry Service, PO Box 71, Milton Keynes MK7 6YZ. Telephone 01908 274066.

## Employment Advice

### Useful Addresses & Telephone Numbers
*ACAS (Advisory, Conciliation and Arbitration Service)* – 27 Wilton Street, London SW1X 7AX. Telephone 0171 388 5100.
*Citizens Advice Bureau* – Look for the local CAB office in your telephone directory. They give free, independent, confidential advice and information on just about anything including employment rights.
*Equal Opportunities Commission* – Overseas House, Quay Street, Manchester M3 3HN. Telephone 0161 833 9244. For advice if you feel you have been discriminated against on grounds of race or sex.
*Free Representation Unit* – 13 Gray's Inn Square, London WC1R 5JP. Telephone 0171 831 0692.
*Redundancy Payments Service* – Free Advice Line: Telephone 0800 848489.

## Pensions, Investments and Financial Planning

### Publications

*A Guide to Savings and Investment* by James Lowlatt (Pan Books).
*Personal Financial Planning Manual* by John Rayer (Butterworth).
*Understanding Your Pension Scheme* by Hancox and MaMahon (Management Update Ltd).

### Useful Addresses & Telephone Numbers

*The Financial Intermediaries, Managers and Brokers Regulatory Association* – Hertsmere House, Hertsmere Road, London E14 4AB. Telephone 0171 538 8860.
*The Society of Pensions Consultants* – Ludgate Circus, London EC4A 2AB. Telephone 0171 353 1688.

## Benefits and Entitlements

### Publications

*Disability Rights Handbook* – Disability Alliance.
*Supplementary Benefits Handbook* – HMSO. Available in public libraries.

### Useful Addresses & Telephone Numbers

*Agency Benefits (NHS Charges)* – Agency Benefits Unit, DSS, Longbenton, Newcastle-upon-Tyne NE98 1YX.
*Enquiries about benefits* – Check in your local telephone book under Social Security.
*General Social Security Advice* – Free Social Security Telephone Helpline: 0800 666555.

*Leaflets and claim forms for benefits* – Leaflets Unit, PO Box 21, Stanmore, Middlesex.
*Unemployment Benefit* – Check in your local telephone book under Unemployment Benefit Office.

A wide range of DSS leaflets can now be viewed on the Internet at http://www.open.gov.uk/dssca/cahome.htm

# Taxation

## Publications

*Self Assessment* – Various guides, videos and a PC floppy disk on completing your tax return available from Tax Enquiry Centres and Tax Offices. Addresses are in your phone book under 'Inland Revenue'. Most offices are open to the public from 9.30am to 4.00pm, Monday to Friday, and some are also open outside these hours.

*The VAT Guide* plus a wide range of leaflets on VAT – Local office of HM Customs and Excise. Details can be found in your phone book under 'Customs and Excise'.

*With Government Approval – A guide to reducing your personal tax bill completely legally* – Sunday Telegraph.

# Health

## Publications

*Better Breathing*, Henryk Hrehorow (Winslow Press).
*Coping with Crisis*, Murgatroyd and Woolfe (Harper and Row).
*Diet 2000*, Dr Allan Maryon Davies (Pan).
*Fitness on Forty Minutes of Exercise a Week*, Carruthers and Murray (Futura).
*Living Well*, The People Maintenance Manual (Michell Beazley).

*Physical Fitness*, Royal Canadian Air Force (Penguin).
*Simple Relaxation*, Laura Mitchell (John Murray).
*Stress and Relaxation*, Jane Madders (Dunitz).
*Take Care of Yourself*, D M Vickery and J F Fries (Allen and Unwin).

# Index

ability tests 175-176
achievements 77-81
advertised vacancies 89-96
advertisements 111-114
advertising:
   internet 96-97
   newspapers, national 89-94
   newspapers, regional 94-95
   trade and professional magazines 95-96
ageism 113
application forms 125-127
application letters 114-125
applications, making speculative 129-135
   speculative letters to employers 132-135
   speculative letters to recruitment specialists 129-131
assessment centres 180-181

body language 164-169

career change (or more of the same) 35-48
   are you in a rut? 38-39
   change to what? 44-48
   employment trends 39-40
   further education 47-48
   finances, examine your 41
   health, your 44
   interim management 45-46
   involving your partner 41
   maturity 40-41
   moving house 42
   new employment 44, 46-46
   salary and benefits 43
   self-assessment 36-38
   self-employment 46
   skills 43-44
   status 42
   temporary employment 45
   voluntary work 45, 46-47
careers – information 195-196
computerised registers 102-103

consultants: 97-100, 129-131, 137-139
  including headhunters, recruitment specialists and recruitment consultants
contractual paperwork 15, 23
curriculum vitae 71-88, 105, 114, 115, 147, 148
  achievements 77-81
  CV's that win interviews 71-74
  leisure interests 82-83
  other useful tips 81-82
  personal profile, the 74-76
  presentation 83-84
  style 79
  technology 84-87

Dos and Don'ts – on the day of the interview 170-172

employee specification 143-145
employment advice – information 203
Employment Protection (Consolidation) Act 1978 11, 16, 24
employment trends 39-40
executive jobclubs 102
ex-gratia payments 25

exhibitions 103

fees, recruitment specialists 100
finance, personal 26-32, 41
  income tax 24-25, 28
  investments 28
  mortgage 27
  pension 27-28
  private health insurance 29
  state benefits 29-32
franchising 192-194
further education 47-48, 202-203

general intelligence tests 177
goals 9
graphology 181-182

headhunters 97-98, 129, 138
health 44, 205-206

income tax 24-25, 28, 205
interim management 45-46, 200
interviews 137-172
  appearance 163-164
  body laguage 164-169
  common interview questions 152-157

employee specifications 143-145
exploratory 141
group 142
interview nerves, controlling 158-164
job descriptions 143
on the day of the interview – Dos and Don'ts 70-172
panel or selection board 141
performance, reviewing your 172
preparing 145-148
techniques, interviewer's questioning 148-154
sequential 141
stress 142
with consultants 137-140
with employers 141-143
your questions 157-158
internet, the 96-97
investments 28

job application progress sheet 62
job centres 22, 23, 24, 29, 30, 31, 188, 196
job descriptions 143
job offers 184-186
job search – information 196
job search seminars 102

jobseekers allowance 29, 30-32
job simulations 181

leisure interests 82-83

maturity 40-41

networking 104, 105-110
  networking letters 106-107
  networking meetings 108-109
  networking techniques 106
  what is networking 105-106
new employment 44, 45-46
newspapers 89-95, 197-200
notice of redundancy 15, 22-23

Open University 40
outplacement 100-101

payments in lieu of notice 24-25
pc information on employers 69
pension 27-28, 204
personal finance 26-32
personal profile 74-76, 83
personality tests 177-178

planning for success 59-64
　disciplined approach 59-60
　equipment 61
　job applicaton progress
　　sheet 62
　office routine 63-64
　setting targets 60
　space of your own 60-61
positive thinking, the
　importance of 7-9
private health insurance 29
professional associations 104

recruitment agencies 100
recruitment consultants 98-
　100, 129
recruitment specialists 97-
　100, 129-131, 137-139
redundancy 11-33
　contractual paperwork 23
　definition 11-12
　Employment Protection
　　(Consolidation) Act 1978
　　11, 16, 24
　feelings you encounter 12-
　　13
　making the most of a
　　difficult situation 14-15
　personal finance 26-32
　problems you might
　　encounter 23-24
　notice of 15, 22-23
　State redundancy
　　payments 16-25
　Statutory Rights 15
　tax 24-25
　time off to look for work
　　25-26
rejection 4, 9, 183-184
researching the job market
　65-69
　Britain's Privately Owned
　　Companies 67
　CBI Directory 69
　The City Directory 68
　Directory of British
　　Associations 66
　identifying potential
　　employers 65-66
　Kelly's Manufacturers and
　　Merchants Directory 68
　Key British Companies 67
　KOMPASS 66-67
　local council directories 69
　Major Companies in
　　Europe 68
　McCathy UK Quoted &
　　Unquoted Service 68
　pc information on
　　employers 69
　The Personnel Manager's
　　Yearbook 68
　Stock Exchange Official
　　Yearbook 67

The Times 1000 67
Who Owns Whom 67

salary and benefits 43
selection methods, other 173-182
  assessment centres 180-181
  graphology 181-182
  job simulations 181
selection tests 173-180
  a brief history 173-174
  what are they? 174-175
  types: ability 175-178
  general intelligence 177
  personality 177-178
  preparing a test strategy 179-181
self-assessment 36-38
self employment 46, 200-201
sequential interviews 141
skills 43-44, 49-54
sources of information, useful 195-206
state benefits 29-32, 204-205
state redundancy payments 16-25
status 42
statutory rights 15
strengths and weaknesses 8, 54-55
stress interviews 142

taking care of yourself 26
technology (in selection) 84-87
tv and radio advertising 104
temporary employment 45
trade and professional magazines 95-96
Training and Enterprise Councils 188

vacanies – how to find them 89-104
  advertised vacancies 89-96
  computerised registers 102-103
  executive Jobclubs 102
  exhibitions 103
  fees 100
  headhunters 97-98
  jobcentres 101-102
  job search seminars 102
  networking 104
  newspapers 89-95
  outplacement services 100-101
  professional associations 104
  recruitment agencies 100
  recruitment consultants 98-99
  tv and radio 104

vacancies, responding to advertised 111-128
  advertisements, what to look for in 111-114
  ageism 113
  application forms 125-127
  application letters 114-125
voluntary sector 202
voluntary work 45, 46-47

working for yourself 187-194
  advice and guidance 18
  business plan, the 189
  do you have what it takes? 187-188
  franchising 192-194
  legal identities 189-192